Intentional Choices:

discovering contentment in stressful times

Bible Study That Builds Christian Community

SERENDIPITY
HOUSE

LIFE
CONNECTIONS

Intentional Choices: Discovering Contentment in Stressful Times
Group Member Book
© 2001, 2003 Serendipity House
Reprinted May 2005

Published by Serendipity House Publishers
Nashville, Tennessee

ISBN: 1-5749-4068-6

Dewey Decimal Classification: 155.9
Subject Headings:
STRESS (PSYCHOLOGY) \ MENTAL HEALTH

Unless otherwise indicated, all Scripture quotations are taken from *The Holy Bible, New International Version®. NIV®.* Copyright © 1973, 1978, 1984 by International Bible Society. Used by permission of Zondervan Publishing House. All rights reserved.

To purchase additional copies of this resource or other studies:
ORDER ONLINE at www.SerendipityHouse.com
WRITE Serendipity House, 117 10th Avenue North, Nashville, TN 37234
FAX (615) 277-8181
PHONE (800) 525-9563

1-800-525-9563
www.SerendipityHouse.com

Printed in the United States of America
10 09 08 07 06 05   4 5 6 7 8 9 10 11

Contents

Core Values

Community: The purpose of this curriculum is to build community within the body of believers around Jesus Christ.

Group Process: To build community, the curriculum must be designed to take a group through a step-by-step process of sharing your story with one another.

Interactive Bible Study: To share your "story," the approach to Scripture in the curriculum needs to be open-ended and right-brained—to "level the playing field" and encourage everyone to share.

Developmental Stages: To provide a healthy program in the life cycle of a group, the curriculum needs to offer courses on three levels of commitment:

(1) Beginner Level—low-level entry, high structure, to level the playing field;
(2) Growth Level—deeper Bible study, flexible structure, to encourage group accountability;
(3) Discipleship Level—in-depth Bible study, open structure, to move the group into high gear.

Target Audiences: To build community throughout the culture of the church, the curriculum needs to be flexible, adaptable, and transferable into the structure of the average church.

Mission: To expand the kingdom of God one person at a time by filling the "empty chair." (We add an extra chair to each group session to remind us of our mission.)

Group Covenant

It is important that your group covenant together, agreeing to live out important group values. Once these values are agreed upon, your group will be on its way to experiencing Christian community. It's very important that your group discuss these values—preferably as you begin this study. The first session would be most appropriate. (Check the rules to which each member of your group agrees.)

- ☐ **Priority:** While you are in this course of study, you give the group meetings priority.
- ☐ **Participation:** Everyone is encouraged to participate and no one dominates.
- ☐ **Respect:** Everyone is given the right to his or her own opinion, and all questions are encouraged and respected.
- ☐ **Confidentiality:** Anything that is said in the meeting is never repeated outside the meeting.
- ☐ **Life Change:** We will regularly assess our own life-change goals and encourage one another in our pursuit of Christlikeness.
- ☐ **Empty Chair:** The group stays open to reaching new people at every meeting.
- ☐ **Care and Support:** Permission is given to call upon each other at any time, especially in times of crisis. The group will provide care for every member.
- ☐ **Accountability:** We agree to let the members of the group hold us accountable to the commitments we make in whatever loving ways we decide upon.
- ☐ **Mission:** We will do everything in our power to start a new group.
- ☐ **Ministry:** The group will encourage one another to volunteer and serve in a ministry and to support missions by giving financially and/or personally serving.

notes

1

The Stress of Anxious Anticipation

Prepare for the Session

	READINGS	REFLECTIVE QUESTIONS
Monday	Philippians 4:4	What can keep you from rejoicing in the Lord at all times?
Tuesday	Psalm 118:24	What are some good things about today? Thank God for them. What are some worries? Pray about them.
Wednesday	Philippians 4:5	Who could you surprise with gentleness today?
Thursday	Matthew 6:25–34	Underline one verse from this passage that speaks to you today. Why did you select it?
Friday	Mark 14:32–34	When have you, like Jesus, dreaded the events of the coming day? How did Jesus cope with this situation?
Saturday	1 Peter 5:7	What worry or anxiety have you "cast" to Jesus, only to reel it back in? Pray about that worry and reflect on how much Jesus loves you.
Sunday	Philippians 4:6–7	Where in your life do you need "the peace of God, which transcends all understanding"? How would it change your current thoughts and actions?

BIBLE STUDY

- to understand that prayer is God's prescription for diffusing anxiety
- to recognize the importance of hearing God speak in the midst of our anxiety
- to realize where the prayer burden must be placed to cast off worry and anxiety

LIFE CHANGE

- to identify our surface and root worries and acknowledge them to God
- to read the Bible and select two of the promises of God to memorize
- to prepare a plan of action and prayer, then leave the rest to God

Icebreaker

10-15 minutes

Worry Barometer. Which of the following statements would cause you the greatest worry and stress?

- ☐ Your dentist saying, "I think we're looking at a root canal."
- ☐ Your daughter saying, "Before you see the car, let me explain."
- ☐ Your in-laws saying, "We'll just be staying for a week or so."
- ☐ Your wife saying, "Let's re-do the bathroom ourselves."
- ☐ Your husband saying, "I'm thinking of getting a motorcycle."
- ☐ Your boss saying, "Come in and close the door."
- ☐ Your best friend saying, "What would you think about me going out with your ex-fiance?"
- ☐ Your mother saying, "He seemed so nice I gave him your phone number."
- ☐ Your father saying, "We're looking at that house for sale on your street."
- ☐ Your hairdresser saying, "I'm moving to Baltimore."
- ☐ Your son saying, "I think I'd like to be a hairdresser."
- ☐ Your wife saying, "The construction crew cut the cable lines. We won't have TV for a week."

Bible Study

30-45 minutes

The Scripture for this week:

LEARNING FROM THE BIBLE

PHILIPPIANS 4:4–7

⁴Rejoice in the Lord always. I will say it again: Rejoice! ⁵Let your gentleness be evident to all. The Lord is near. ⁶Do not be anxious about anything, but in everything, by prayer and petition, with thanksgiving, present your requests to God. ⁷And the peace of God, which transcends all understanding, will guard your hearts and your minds in Christ Jesus.

...about today's session

A WORD FROM THE LEADER

1. What is developing in our society along with rapid technological advancement?

Write your answers here.

2. What gives Paul exceptional credibility as he advises us on confronting worry?

Identifying with the Story

♘ In horseshoe groups of 6–8, explore questions as time allows.

1. Life is often a three-ring circus of major concerns. From the following areas, rank your top three concerns according to what is provoking the most worry in your life at this time.

   ___ finances   ___ children
   ___ career   ___ ex-spouse
   ___ spouse   ___ family member
   ___ parent(s)   ___ a difficult decision
   ___ health   ___ other: _____

2. Finish this sentence with one of the choices that follow: "My approach to worry is to ..."

◯ lie awake at night and imagine the worst
◯ attack it with busyness
◯ smother the worry with chocolate
◯ force myself to think rationally about the issue
◯ pray, pray, pray
◯ distract myself with entertainment
◯ upgrade to a panic attack
◯ talk it out and get feedback
◯ other: _____

3. Which of the following is the best metaphor for your experience of prayer?

◯ fast food   ◯ Lean Cuisine
◯ junk food   ◯ gourmet meal
◯ leftover lasagna   ◯ Slim-Fast
◯ all-you-can-eat buffet

today's session

1. Paul's words in Philippians 4:6 are not so much a condemnation of worry as a _____ for dealing with worry.

2. The English translation of the Greek word *merimnao* is: _____. The English word taken from *phroneo* is:_____.

3. The phrase translated into English from Philippians 2:20, "takes a genuine interest" and the word translated "concern" in 2 Corinthians 11:28 are both found to contain the Greek word for _____.

4. What is the best thing we can do when we're anxious?

5. What role does hearing God play in reducing worry?

6. According to this passage, if my worry is to be restrained, who must do the praying?

Learning from the Story

In horseshoe groups of 6–8, choose an answer and explain why you chose what you did.

1. What is the difference between anxiety and concern? How do the Greek words *merimnao* and *phroneo* illustrate this in Scripture?

2. What was the most beneficial insight about prayer that you gained today?

   ☐ Worry is a signal to start praying.
   ☐ Genuine prayer isn't just about talking; it's also about listening.
   ☐ In the Garden of Gethsemane, what Jesus heard was perhaps more important than what He said.
   ☐ I must pray for myself in order to diffuse my worry.
   ☐ Peace is the result of genuine prayer.
   ☐ Other: _____

life change lessons

How can you apply this session to your life?

Write your answers here.

1. What are the two types of worry you should identify and acknowledge to God?

2. In order to attack worry, what must you hear and rehearse?

3. What does worry empty today of?

Caring Time

15-20 minutes

This is the time for developing and expressing your caring for group members. Take turns praying for the concerns listed on the Prayer/Praise Report, as well as other requests that have been shared. In addition, pray that each group member will find peace through prayer.

If you would like to pray silently, say "Amen" when you have finished so the next person will know when to start.

Pray specifically for God to guide you to someone to invite next week.

Reference Notes

Use these notes to gain further understanding
of the text as you study on your own.

Rejoice in the Lord always. Following an exhortation to the Philippians to be unified, and citing a specific case of division that concerns him, Paul proceeds to encourage the development of positive Christian behaviors. First, believers are to rejoice—to be filled with and express joy. Note that the exhortation is to rejoice *in the Lord*. It is faith in Christ and a focus on His love, grace, and goodness that makes joyfulness realistic and possible. It is this perspective that allows Paul to rejoice in the Lord, though imprisoned.

PHILIPPIANS 4:4 (cont'd)

I will say it again: Rejoice! Paul repeats the admonition for emphasis. An additional purpose of the repetition is likely a response to the skeptical reaction to his first exclamation. Facing great difficulty themselves and with their leader in prison, the Philippians would likely greet his joyful advice with disbelief or reluctance. The repetition is Paul's way of saying, "Yes, you heard me right; rejoice, I tell you!"

PHILIPPIANS 4:5

gentleness. The Greek word, *epiekes*, describes a willingness to yield one's personal rights when the normal or expected response would be retaliation (see Matt. 5:38–42).

The Lord is near. This is not referring to Christ's continual presence but to His second coming, at which time the righteous Judge will confront all injustices.

PHILIPPIANS 4:6

Do not be anxious. The Greek word, *merimnao*, implies excessive concern or anxiety. The verb tense suggests continual anxiety. In other words, "Do not be constantly anxious about anything." In context with the preceding verses, Paul is specifically admonishing the Philippians not to worry about the problems of present or future persecution. However, since Paul said that believers should not be anxious about *anything*, certainly the application may be extended beyond the experiences of persecution.

prayer and petition, with thanksgiving. Prayer, *proseuche*, implies the attitude of worship. Petition, *deesei*, is the expression of needs. Thanksgiving, *eucharistias*, should accompany all prayer.

PHILIPPIANS 4:7

the peace of God. This is the only time this phrase is used in the New Testament. Note that the prayerful and obedient believer is promised the peace of God (v. 7) and the God of peace (Phil. 4:9).

transcends all understanding. It is a supernatural peace that cannot be explained by logic or attained by good psychology. It is a peace that operates not in a denial of reality, but transcends circumstances.

guard your hearts and your minds. Drawing from a military analogy, to guard, *phroureo*, recalls a military garrison stationed inside the city, employed to protect its citizens. Thus, the peace of God residing within the heart and mind of the praying believer acts as a guard against intruding anxious thoughts.

notes

2

The Stress of
Making Mistakes

Prepare for the Session

	READINGS	REFLECTIVE QUESTIONS
Monday	Matthew 26:17–30	How do you react when someone betrays you? How did Jesus react to Judas' betrayal?
Tuesday	Matthew 26:31–34	How do you think you would have responded if Jesus predicted *your* falling away?
Wednesday	Matthew 26:35	Under what circumstances might you be willing to die for Christ?
Thursday	Matthew 26:69–72	In whose presence this past week did you downplayed your identity as a follower of Christ?
Friday	Matthew 26:73–74	Recall a time when you made a commitment or recommitment that didn't last very long. How did you feel?
Saturday	Luke 22:61	What do you imagine Jesus communicated through His facial expression when He looked at Peter?
Sunday	Matthew 26:75	Recall a time when you were overwhelmed by a feeling of failure. What helped get you through that difficult time?

BIBLE STUDY
- to realize that God anticipates our failures
- to recognize that God believes in us in spite of our failures
- to celebrate the fact that God forgives our failures

LIFE CHANGE
- to make a list of our failures and confess them to God
- to write down what we learned and how to make future adjustments for each failure on our lists
- to seek an accountability partner who will give us encouragement and help us minimize future failures

Icebreaker

10-15 minutes

Penalties, Turnovers, and Bloopers. Which of the following best describes one of your recent mistakes?

☐ FUMBLE—I was taking a lot of hits and eventually I messed up.

☐ CENTER FIELD COLLISION—I think I may have hurt someone on my team.

☐ OFFSIDES—I responded hastily.

☐ TECHNICAL FOUL—I said something I should not have said.

☐ DELAY OF GAME—I didn't plan my time very well and didn't get the job done.

☐ HOLE IN MY GLOVE—I don't know how it happened.

☐ BLOWN LAY-UP—I must have lost concentration.

☐ Other: _____

Information to Remember: In the spaces provided, take note of information you will need as you participate in this group in the weeks to come.

PEOPLE:

1. A person here I don't know yet is:

2. Something I can do to get acquainted with this person is:

EVENTS: An event that is coming up that I want to make sure I am part of is _____. It will be _____ (time) on _____ (date) at _____ (location).

And if I have time, I would also like to be part of _____. It will be _____ (time) on _____ (date) at _____ (location).

LEARNING
FROM THE
BIBLE

Bible Study

30-45 minutes

The Scripture for this week:

**MATTHEW
26:31–35**

³¹*Jesus told them, "This very night you will all fall away on account of me, for it is written:*

"I will strike the shepherd,
and the sheep of the flock will be scattered.'

³²*But after I have risen, I will go ahead of you into Galilee."*
³³*Peter replied, "Even if all fall away on account of you, I never will."*
³⁴*"I tell you the truth," Jesus answered, "this very night, before the rooster crows, you will disown me three times."*
³⁵*But Peter declared, "Even if I have to die with you, I will never disown you." And all the other disciples said the same. ...*

**MATTHEW
26:69–75**

⁶⁹*Peter was sitting out in the courtyard, and a servant girl came to him. "You also were with Jesus of Galilee," she said.*
⁷⁰*But he denied it before them all. "I don't know what you're talking about," he said.*

⁷¹Then he went out to the gateway, where another girl saw him and said to the people there, "This fellow was with Jesus of Nazareth."

⁷²He denied it again, with an oath: "I don't know the man!"

⁷³After a little while, those standing there went up to Peter and said, "Surely you are one of them, for your accent gives you away."

⁷⁴Then he began to call down curses on himself and he swore to them, "I don't know the man!"

Immediately a rooster crowed. ⁷⁵Then Peter remembered the word Jesus had spoken: "Before the rooster crows, you will disown me three times." And he went outside and wept bitterly.

...about today's session

1. What is one of the main reasons that failure produces stress?

2. What are some of the losses that failure may bring?

Identifying with the Story

1. Most recently, in which of the following situations would you have gladly taken a "mulligan"?

   ◯ relating to my spouse
   ◯ relating to my children
   ◯ relating to my parents
   ◯ relating to a friend
   ◯ responding to temptation
   ◯ responding to pressure
   ◯ responding to frustration
   ◯ making a decision
   ◯ dealing with something at work
   ◯ other: _____

2. Complete the following sentence: "I'm most likely to downplay my relationship to Christ when I am with ..."

- ☐ my parent(s)
- ☐ my in-law(s)
- ☐ my neighbors
- ☐ my coworkers
- ☐ my customers/clients
- ☐ a potential date
- ☐ other: _____

3. If you knew that being identified as a Christian might threaten your job security, financial security, family's safety, your health, or even your life, how courageous do you think you'd be in standing up for Christ? What if you were threatened with death if you did not renounce Christ?

today's session

What is God teaching you from this story?

1. While Jesus does not affirm our failures, He does _____ them.

2. From Luke 22:31–32, we are relieved to learn that Jesus _____ in us despite our failures. What in the passage indicates this truth?

3. How would you describe Jesus' probable expression when He "looked straight at Peter"?

4. The message that Peter received after Christ's resurrection encourages us that Jesus _____ our failures.

5. What happens when God forgives, in addition to a pardon of sin and a removal of the penalty?

Learning from the Story

1. What do you think Peter's greatest failure was?

   ☐ misunderstanding the reason for Jesus' declaration about scattered sheep
   ☐ overestimating his own courage
   ☐ making a grand rededication and pledge of loyalty instead of asking for help
   ☐ allowing a servant girl to intimidate him
   ☐ stooping to such forceful denial
   ☐ other: _____

2. How do you think you'd respond to Jesus if He said to *you*, "Satan has asked to sift you as wheat, but I've prayed for you that your faith may not fail, and after you've turned back strengthen your brothers and sisters"?

   ☐ "Just because Satan asked, you didn't have to give him permission."
   ☐ (gulp) "What will this sifting be like ... exactly?"
   ☐ "Bring him on, I'm ready for him. We'll see who gets sifted!"
   ☐ "What do you mean by 'after I've turned back'?"
   ☐ "Can he sift me if I don't get out of bed?"
   ☐ "Just how weak can my faith be before you'd say it failed?"
   ☐ "Well, if you've prayed for me then I'll be all right, won't I?"

3. If you know that God offers forgiveness for failure, what is your incentive to avoid failure?

☐ I want to please God.
☐ I still believe that obedience brings greater blessing.
☐ I don't want to sabotage my testimony.
☐ I'd rather by-pass the guilt right from the outset.
☐ I'd prefer to avoid the consequences of failure.
☐ Other: _____

2

life change lessons

How can you apply this session to your life?

Write your answers here.

1. What is the first thing to do when failures occur?

2. How can failure provide a valuable education?

3. What is a radical way to minimize future failure?

Caring Time

15-20 minutes

CARING TIME

♘ **Remain in horseshoe groups of 6–8.**

Take time now to pray for one another and for your own special concerns. Ask God to help each group member grow and learn from his or her mistakes and failures as Peter did. Also remember to pray for the concerns listed on the Prayer/Praise Report.

Pray specifically for God to guide you to someone to invite next week to fill the empty chair.

Close by thanking God for bringing you together as a group and by asking Him to help you understand and grow spiritually.

BIBLE STUDY NOTES

Reference Notes

Use these notes to gain further understanding
of the text as you study on your own.

MATTHEW 26:31

fall away on account of me. Because of Jesus' suffering, the disciples would distance themselves from Him out of fear for their own safety.

I will strike the shepherd. Jesus is quoting Zechariah 13:7. He is not condemning or shaming His disciples, but He is pointing out that what seems like chaos is actually part of God's master plan.

MATTHEW 26:32

go ahead of you into Galilee. Jesus is arranging a reunion after His resurrection. Not only is He giving them the location, but He is again implying His forgiveness. "Although you will forsake me, I will not forsake you."

MATTHEW 26:35

I will never disown you. Peter challenges the accuracy of Jesus' prophecy and declares that his loyalty, bravery, and commitment to Jesus will prove to at least match, if not exceed, that of any other disciple.

MATTHEW 26:69

sitting out in the courtyard. Peter did not flee in the opposite direction but followed the arresting mob at a comfortable distance. Upon arriving at the courtyard of the high priest, he sought to blend in with the crowd (Matt. 26:58).

MATTHEW 26:70

denied it. Peter's first denial was an attempt at being evasive, also known as "playing dumb."

MATTHEW 26:72   *denied it again, with an oath.* His second reply was a firm denial under oath.

MATTHEW 26:74   *began to call down curses on himself.* In his third level of denial, Peter called down curses upon himself if he were lying. The use of the word "began" implies that he continued this for some time, probably from one person to another. Following this third series of denials, the rooster crows in fulfillment of Jesus' prophecy.

MATTHEW 26:75   *Peter remembered the word.* The sound of the crowing rooster was like a siren that silenced Peter and reminded him of Jesus' prediction concerning him.

went outside and wept bitterly. Peter fled from the crowd and privately collapsed in loud sobbing.

notes

The Stress of Relationships

Prepare for the Session

	READINGS	REFLECTIVE QUESTIONS
Monday	Joshua 22:9–12	When have you jumped to the wrong conclusion about someone? How did that affect your relationship?
Tuesday	Joshua 22:13–20	Who do you need to talk to about a conflict you're having? Take time to pray for that person.
Wednesday	Joshua 22:21–29	How do you usually respond when someone confronts you? How would you like to change?
Thursday	Joshua 22:30–34	Praise God for the special relationships He has given you.
Friday	Matthew 5:43–48	Who do you find most difficult to love? How could you show Jesus' love to that person?
Saturday	Acts 15:36–41	Have you ever parted ways with someone over a disagreement? How does it make you feel to know that Paul had disagreements, too?
Sunday	Philippians 4:2–3	What is Paul's ultimate concern about the conflict here?

BIBLE STUDY · to realize that unity is not the absence of conflict but the result of resolved conflict
· to recognize that resolution is not possible without communication
· to understand that reconciliation is not gained without cooperation

LIFE CHANGE · to pray about current conflicts and ask for wisdom and discernment in clarifying our impressions
· to choose one strained relationship and begin seeking resolution or reconciliation this week
· to accept the occasional limitations of reconciliation

Icebreaker

10-15 minutes

**GATHERING
THE PEOPLE
◊ Form
horseshoe
groups of 6–8.**

Cartoon Conflicts. Which of the following comic strips best reflects the source of a recent conflict you've experienced?

☐ Dilbert (coworkers, boss, company)
☐ Calvin & Hobbs (child)
☐ Cathy (boyfriend, girlfriend, parents)
☐ Peanuts (friends)
☐ Sally Forth (spouse, child)
☐ Ziggy (myself)
☐ Far Side (alien from outer space or ex-spouse)
☐ Other: _____

Information to Remember: In the spaces provided, take note of information you will need as you participate in this group in the weeks to come.

PEOPLE:

1. A person in the group, besides the leader, I learned from this week was:

2. A person who lifted my spirits was:

EVENTS: An event that is coming up that I want to make sure I am part of is _____. It will be _____ (time) on _____ (date) at _____ (location).

And if I have time, I would also like to be part of _____. It will be _____ (time) on _____ (date) at _____ (location).

Bible Study

30-45 minutes

The Scripture for this week:

**JOSHUA
22:15–18**

¹⁵When they went to Gilead—to Reuben, Gad and the half-tribe of Manasseh—they said to them: ¹⁶"The whole assembly of the Lord says: 'How could you break faith with the God of Israel like this? How could you turn away from the Lord and build yourselves an altar in rebellion against him now? ¹⁷Was not the sin of Peor enough for us? Up to this very day we have not cleansed ourselves from that sin, even though a plague fell on the community of the Lord! ¹⁸And are you now turning away from the Lord?

" 'If you rebel against the Lord today, tomorrow he will be angry with the whole community of Israel. ...

**JOSHUA
22:21–27**

²¹Then Reuben, Gad and the half-tribe of Manasseh replied to the heads of the clans of Israel: ²²"The Mighty One, God, the Lord! The Mighty One, God, the Lord! He knows! And let Israel know! If this has been in rebellion or disobedience to the Lord, do not spare us this day. ²³If we have built our own altar to turn away from the Lord and to offer burnt offerings and grain offerings, or to sacrifice fellowship offerings on it, may the Lord himself call us to account.

²⁴"No! We did it for fear that some day your descendants might say to ours, 'What do you have to do with the Lord, the God of Israel? ²⁵The Lord has made the Jordan a boundary between us and you—you Reubenites and Gadites! You have no share in the Lord.' So your descendants might cause ours to stop fearing the Lord.

²⁶"That is why we said, 'Let us get ready and build an altar—but not for burnt offerings or sacrifices.' ²⁷On the contrary, it is to be a witness between us and you and the generations that follow, that we will worship the Lord at his sanctuary with our burnt offerings, sacrifices and fellowship offerings. Then in the future your descendants will not be able to say to ours, 'You have no share in the Lord.' ...

JOSHUA 22:32–34

³²Then Phinehas son of Eleazar, the priest, and the leaders returned to Canaan from their meeting with the Reubenites and Gadites in Gilead and reported to the Israelites. ³³They were glad to hear the report and praised God. And they talked no more about going to war against them to devastate the country where the Reubenites and the Gadites lived.

³⁴And the Reubenites and the Gadites gave the altar this name: A Witness Between Us that the Lord is God.

...about today's session

A WORD FROM THE LEADER

Write your answers here.

1. How can it be said that the Bible is a book of conflict?

2. Why is conflict practically inevitable in relationships?

Identifying with the Story

In horseshoe groups of 6–8, explore questions as time allows.

1. Conflict is often the result of a misunderstanding or misinterpretation. With whom has your most recent conflict been caused by a misunderstanding or misinterpretation?

   ☐ spouse
   ☐ boyfriend/girlfriend
   ☐ friend
   ☐ family member
   ☐ child
   ☐ coworker or boss

2. What was the root cause of the misunderstanding or conflict?

   ☐ I believed and acted upon someone else's report.
   ☐ I failed to check out my assumption.
   ☐ I acted on the basis of the person's past behavior.
   ☐ I misread the nonverbals.
   ☐ I didn't offer the benefit of a doubt.
   ☐ I operated by "guilty until proven innocent."
   ☐ I probably wanted to believe the worst.
   ☐ I didn't bother to check with other sources before I confronted someone.
   ☐ Other: _____

3. Which of the following best illustrates your style of dealing with conflict?

   ☐ lion—attack first
   ☐ turtle—turn inward and be silent
   ☐ bird—flee
   ☐ skunk—fight dirty
   ☐ chameleon—acquiesce
   ☐ bear—attack if threatened
   ☐ snake—attack when least expected
   ☐ puppy—whimper and cry
   ☐ peacock—make a scene
   ☐ other: _____

3

What is God teaching you from this story?

1. What is the expected by-product of differences? What are some of the many differences we bring to the table in relationships?

2. Unity is not the _____ of conflict but the result of _____ conflict.

3. Faulty _____ almost always leads to flawed _____ that provoke wrong _____ with potentially disastrous _____.

4. Resolution is not possible without _____.

5. Good conflict resolution always begins with _____ rather than _____.

6. Reconciliation is not possible without _____.

Learning from the Story

⊍ In horseshoe groups of 6–8, choose an answer and explain why you chose what you did.

1. Which of the following differences played a role in a recent conflict you experienced? Check all that apply.

- ☐ personality
- ☐ background
- ☐ experiences
- ☐ expectations
- ☐ perception
- ☐ values
- ☐ beliefs
- ☐ goals
- ☐ convictions
- ☐ other:_____

2. How would you grade yourself on your ability to deal constructively with conflict?

A+   A   A-   B+   B   B-   C+   C   C-   D+   D   D-   F

3. What negative example can you learn from the conflict in today's passage? What positive example can you learn?

life change lessons

How can you apply this session to your life?

Write your answers here.

1. What is a positive, gentle way to introduce a concern?

2. What should be your two goals in conflict resolution?

3. Your _____ for conflict will determine your _____ of conflict.

4. What should you do when someone repeatedly resists your attempts at peacemaking?

Caring Time

CARING TIME

⋃ **Remain in horseshoe groups of 6–8.**

Remember that this is the time to express your caring for each other and to support one another in prayer. Pray that God will help each of you to handle conflicts with a spirit of resolution and reconciliation. Also pray for the concerns listed on the Prayer/Praise Report.

Pray specifically for God to guide you to someone to invite for next week to fill the empty chair.

Close by giving each group member a few minutes to say a prayer of thanksgiving for the special relationships God has graciously and lovingly given to him or her.

BIBLE STUDY NOTES

Reference Notes

Use these notes to gain further understanding
of the text as you study on your own.

This account quickly moves from the affirmation that God's will was accomplished in all that Israel did (Josh. 21:43–45), to the resolution of the first challenge to that statement. In Joshua 22:1–6, the division of the promised land is completed. Joshua delivers an affirmation, an exhortation of continued obedience, blesses the tribes, and sends them to their new homes.

JOSHUA 22:15

Reuben, Gad and the half-tribe of Manasseh. The Reubenites were descendants of Reuben, Jacob's son. (He did not become famous for inventing the deli sandwich!) The tribe of Gad or Gadites were descendants of Jacob's servant son, Gad, and were the 8th largest of the 12 tribes that came out of Egypt. They were cattlemen and had a reputation for fierceness in battle. The tribe of Manasseh traced its origins back to Joseph's oldest son Manasseh. This was a very large tribe that divided itself into two tribes and settled on opposite sides of the Jordan. The division was harmonious and not due to any conflict.

break faith. This was the same root word used to describe Achan's sin of defying the Lord's command in Joshua 7.

sin of Peor. Some of the Israelites participated in the Moabite worship of the Baal of Peor (Num. 25:1–5). God's judgment of this flagrant idolatry cost 24,000 people their lives in a plague.

he will be angry with the whole community. The western tribes are concerned for their own safety, fearing that God will judge the entire nation for the rebellion of the eastern tribes. Again, the example of Achan's sin is used in verse 20.

your descendants will not be able to say to ours, "You have no share in the Lord" (v. 27). The eastern tribes explain their reasoning: In case false information is circulated over time among the western tribes as to the reason for the eastern tribes' location, the altar would serve as a constant, visual, and corrective statement. The eastern tribes were reinforcing their allegiance to God and their right to worship Him at the tabernacle at Shiloh (on the west side).

notes

4

The Stress of Loss

Prepare for the Session

4

	READINGS	REFLECTIVE QUESTIONS
Monday	Job 1:6–15	When have you had to tell someone bad news? How did you do it?
Tuesday	Job 1:18–22	Looking back, how have you handled grief in your life?
Wednesday	Psalm 31:9–10	Have you ever felt like David did when he wrote this psalm? What made you feel that way?
Thursday	2 Samuel 1:17–27	In what positive way did David deal with his grief in this situation?
Friday	John 16:19–22	What do you find most comforting in this passage?
Saturday	Matthew 5:4	How can you comfort someone who is mourning today?
Sunday	1 Thessalonians 4:13–18	How is the Christian's grief to be different from the "rest of man"?

BIBLE STUDY   · to understand the dynamics of grief
                          · to recognize the unhealthy responses to grief
                          · to accept the healthy responses to grief

LIFE CHANGE   · to accept our grief
                          · to limit our grief
                          · to redeem our grief

Icebreaker

10-15 minutes

Lost and Found. Take turns going around the group and answering the first question. Then go around again on the second question, etc.

1. What toy or other item from your childhood do you wish you had kept because it is now considered valuable?

2. What personal possession that has been lost or misplaced do you wish you could find?

3. What possession did you once lose and then happily find?

Information to Remember: Finish the following sentences as you look around at the people here today.

1. The person in the group with the biggest smile today is:

2. A person who has a look of concern on his or her face, and who I should check out after class is:

Bible Study

30-45 minutes

The Scripture for this week:

⁶*One day the angels came to present themselves before the Lord, and Satan also came with them.* ⁷*The Lord said to Satan, "Where have you come from?"*

Satan answered the Lord, "From roaming through the earth and going back and forth in it."

⁸*Then the Lord said to Satan, "Have you considered my servant Job? There is no one on earth like him; he is blameless and upright, a man who fears God and shuns evil."*

⁹*"Does Job fear God for nothing?" Satan replied.* ¹⁰*"Have you not put a hedge around him and his household and everything he has? You have blessed the work of his hands, so that his flocks and herds are spread throughout the land.* ¹¹*But stretch out your hand and strike everything he has, and he will surely curse you to your face."*

¹²*The Lord said to Satan, "Very well, then, everything he has is in your hands, but on the man himself do not lay a finger."*

Then Satan went out from the presence of the Lord.

¹³*One day when Job's sons and daughters were feasting and drinking wine at the oldest brother's house,* ¹⁴*a messenger came to Job and said, "The oxen were plowing and the donkeys were grazing nearby,* ¹⁵*and the Sabeans attacked and carried them off. They put the servants to the sword, and I am the only one who has escaped to tell you!"* …

¹⁸*While he was still speaking, yet another messenger came and said, "Your sons and daughters were feasting and drinking wine at the oldest brother's house,* ¹⁹*when suddenly a mighty wind swept in from the desert and struck the four corners of the house. It collapsed on them and they are dead, and I am the only one who has escaped to tell you!"*

²⁰*At this, Job got up and tore his robe and shaved his head. Then he fell to the ground in worship* ²¹*and said:*

> *"Naked I came from my mother's womb,*
> *and naked I will depart.*
> *The Lord gave and the Lord has taken away;*
> *may the name of the Lord be praised."*

²²*In all this, Job did not sin by charging God with wrongdoing.*

4

...about today's session

A WORD
FROM THE
LEADER

Write your
answers
here.

1. What are some common losses that create stress?

Identifying with the Story

⚘ In
horseshoe
groups
of 6–8,
explore
questions as
time allows.

1. How do you feel about Satan receiving permission to attack Job?

2. What is your reaction to the magnitude of Job's loss?

- ☐ I think it was totally unfair.
- ☐ I think I'd be suicidal.
- ☐ I think God has the right to do anything He wants.
- ☐ I can't comprehend what such loss would feel like.
- ☐ I think I'd be really mad at God.
- ☐ Other: _____

3. What is your opinion of Job's response in verses 20–21?

1. What is a possible or at least partial explanation of Job's response in Job 1:20–21?

2. The five most commonly proposed stages of grief are:

_____

_____

_____

_____

_____

4

3. In unhealthy grieving we are at risk of remaining immobilized by these three false beliefs:

   a. _____, not God, is the source of life, happiness, and fulfillment.

   b. "Because I lost 'X,' my life has nothing of any _____ in it."

   c. "If God _____ me, 'X' would not have happened. He's _____; He could have prevented it."

4. How is healthy grief described here?

Learning from the Story

⌒ In horseshoe groups of 6–8, choose an answer and explain why you chose what you did.

1. Which of the following losses have you experienced in the past five years?

   ☐ loss of relationship by death
   ☐ loss of relationship by separation (break-up, divorce, relocation)
   ☐ loss of job and financial security
   ☐ loss of health
   ☐ loss of dream or goal
   ☐ loss of reputation, status, or approval
   ☐ other: _____

2. Which of these myths did you believe prior to today's session?

   ☐ Grief (or prolonged grief) demonstrates a lack of faith.
   ☐ Mourners need only to express their feelings to resolve grief.
   ☐ To get past grief you must put the loss out of your mind.
   ☐ Mourning should not last more than three months and certainly not more than a year.
   ☐ Grief tapers off evenly and predictably with time.
   ☐ The intensity and duration of mourning reflects the measure of love.
   ☐ Other: _____

3. What is the primary indication that grief is unhealthy?

4. Which of the following best illustrates your style of grieving?

   ☐ calm—like Job in chapter 1
   ☐ explosive—like Job in chapter 3
   ☐ expressive—like David grieving over Jonathan
   ☐ silent and private—like Jesus grieving John's death
   ☐ other: _____

How can you apply this session to your life?

Write your answers here.

1. What does it mean to "accept your grief"?

2. What does it mean to "limit your grief"?

3. What are some ways you can "redeem your grief"?

4

Caring Time

15-20 minutes

CARING TIME

⚘ **Remain in horseshoe groups of 6–8.**

Close by praying for one another. Pray especially for those group members who are going through a time of grief and loss. Also pray for the concerns on the Prayer/Praise Report.

Pray specifically for God to guide you to someone to invite next week to fill the empty chair.

Conclude your prayer time by reading together Jesus' words in John 16:22,33:

Now is your time of grief, but I will see you again and you will rejoice, and no one will take away your joy....

I have told you these things, so that in me you may have peace. In this world you will have trouble. But take heart! I have overcome the world.

Reference Notes

Use these notes to gain further understanding
of the text as you study on your own.

Job endured two tests: first was the loss of his family and his possessions, then it was the loss of his health. In each test we are shown two scenes, one in heaven and one on the earth. In the heavenly scenes, Satan acts as the accuser, and in the earthly scenes that follow he becomes the assailant.

JOB 1:6   *the angels came to present themselves.* The purpose of presenting themselves to God was, apparently, to report on their activities. Satan also came with the angels and is questioned by God.

JOB 1:7   *roaming through the earth.* This verse reminds us of 1 Peter 5:8 which portrays Satan as a roaring lion on the prowl looking for someone to devour.

JOB 1:8   *my servant Job.* God honors Job by referring to him as "my servant." He also commends him as being blameless ("without moral blemish") and upright ("straight" in the sense of not deviating from God's standards), a man who fears God (has reverence and respect for God), and shuns evil ("turns aside from and puts away evil"). Job is not a sinless man, as he himself admits in 6:24 and 7:21. God, however, honors the bent of his heart and life.

JOB 1:9   *Does Job fear God for nothing?* Here Satan attacks Job's motives. The phrase for nothing (*hinnam*) means "without any reason." Satan does not deny Job's righteous lifestyle; he merely questions his motives for living a godly life. Satan suggests that Job's worship is basically selfish and self-seeking. The entire book of Job, in fact, addresses not only the question of righteous suffering but also the motives for truly worshiping the Lord. Would anyone serve God if there were no personal gain or benefit attached? Is the decision to live uprightly before God simply an effort to place ourselves in the flow of God's present and future blessing, or is it an expression of gratitude for blessings already received? This is the underlying doubt behind Satan's accusations. At the same time, Satan also attacks God's motives for blessing His servant Job. He suggests, in essence, that God is bribing people to worship Him by giving them fortune and health.

JOB 1:12   *everything he has ... but on the man himself.* God allows Satan to strike against Job; however, He puts limits on the attack. Satan's accusations concerning the motives of both Job and the Lord will be answered by Job's response to sudden calamity. The small, single word *but* underscores the truth that all of creation, including Satan, is under God's control and authority.

JOB 1:13   *Job's sons and daughters were feasting.* As described earlier in the chapter, feasting was a common practice of Job's children. Satan chose this normally joyous occasion to unleash a series of four assaults on Job's family and his possessions. These assaults alternated between human attack and destruction by "natural" forces: a Sabean attack (v. 15), "the fire of God" (v. 16), a Chaldean raiding party (v. 17), and a mighty desert wind (v. 19). God permitted Satan to use both sources of damage against Job. The four attacks resulted in devastating losses of the people and the possessions that had been previously described as bountiful blessings in the first few verses of the chapter (seven sons and three daughters, 7,000 sheep, 3,000 camels, 500 yoke of oxen, 500 donkeys, and a large number of servants).

JOB 1:15   *I am the only one ... while he was still speaking.* These two phrases are repeated in each account of the four attacks. They convey both the severe nature of the losses (complete devastation) and the widespread nature of the losses (back-to-back tragedies).

JOB 1:20   *Job ... tore ... shaved ... fell ... in worship.* The tearing of the robe was a sign of inner turmoil and distress. Shaving one's head indicated the loss of personal glory and honor. In spite of all that was taken from him in a moment of time, Job humbly submitted to God's sovereign authority over all things.

JOB 1:21   *may the name of the Lord be praised.* Job's focus was not on created things, but on the Creator, Himself. He acknowledged that he had come into the world with nothing and that he would leave the same way. He recognized and accepted the truth that all life is a gift granted by permission of God. Even amidst his pain and grief, Job did not turn away or even turn against his Lord. Job's incredible response flew in the face of Satan's accusations. God's own description of Job's character proved true as this godly man, stripped of his ten children and all of his possessions, bowed humbly before the Lord in worship.

notes

The Stress of Labor

Prepare for the Session

	READINGS	REFLECTIVE QUESTIONS
Monday	Exodus 5:1–2	How can you be someone who exhibits Christlikeness and tells others about Christ in your workplace?
Tuesday	Exodus 5:10–19	How do you respond when you feel your boss is being unreasonable?
Wednesday	Exodus 5:20–23	What problems are you having at work that you need to talk to God about right now?
Thursday	Luke 5:4–6	Do you ever feel the stress of working hard and seeing few results? How do these words in the Bible encourage you?
Friday	Exodus 4:10–12	How do you need God's help today in fulfilling your job duties?
Saturday	Luke 22:39–44	Take time to pray, as Jesus did, and ask for strength to carry on your work.
Sunday	Colossians 3:22–24	What do these verses say to you about the proper attitude toward the quality of work you do?

BIBLE STUDY
- to understand how our job responsibilities foster stress
- to recognize how the people we work with contribute to stress
- to identify what work conditions promote stress

LIFE CHANGE
- to list the specific sources of our job stress
- to determine reasonable, helpful action steps to reduce the stress
- to evaluate our compatibility with our jobs

Icebreaker

10-15 minutes

**GATHERING
THE PEOPLE
Ⓤ Form
horseshoe
groups of 6–8.**

A New Job Description. Pick two of the following and complete the statements describing a feature of your work. Add your own endings if the ones listed don't fit. Offer a very brief explanation of your answers.

1. My job requires that I:

  ☐ walk on water   ☐ walk a tightrope
  ☐ walk on eggshells   ☐ other: _____

2. My coworkers remind me of:

  ☐ the A-Team   ☐ F-Troop   ☐ Other: _____

3. My boss is:

  ☐ Superman/Superwoman (amazing)
  ☐ Batman/Batwoman (mysterious)
  ☐ The Invisible Man/Woman (inaccessible)
  ☐ Other: _____

4. The atmosphere at work:

  ☐ is hectic as an emergency room
  ☐ is serene as a library
  ☐ changes like the weather
  ☐ other: _____

Information to Remember: In the spaces provided, take note of information you will need as you participate in this group in the weeks to come.

PEOPLE:

1. A person here I would really like to know better is:

2. A person in this group who has really been a blessing to me during these sessions is:

EVENTS: An event that is coming up that I want to make sure I am part of is _____. It will be _____ (time) on _____ (date) at _____ (location).

And if I have time, I would also like to be part of _____. It will be _____ (time) on _____ (date) at _____ (location).

LEARNING FROM THE BIBLE

Bible Study

30-45 minutes

The Scripture for this week:

EXODUS 5:1–2

¹*Afterward Moses and Aaron went to Pharaoh and said, "This is what the Lord, the God of Israel, says: 'Let my people go, so that they may hold a festival to me in the desert.' "*

²*Pharaoh said, "Who is the Lord, that I should obey him and let Israel go? I do not know the Lord and I will not let Israel go." ...*

EXODUS 5:10–23

¹⁰*Then the slave drivers and the foremen went out and said to the people, "This is what Pharaoh says: 'I will not give you any more straw.* ¹¹*Go and get your own straw wherever you can find it, but your work will not be reduced at all.' "* ¹²*So the people scattered all over Egypt to gather stubble to use for straw.* ¹³*The slave drivers kept pressing them, saying, "Complete the work required of you for each day, just as when you had straw."* ¹⁴*The Israelite foremen appointed by Pharaoh's slave drivers were beaten and were asked, "Why didn't you meet your quota of bricks yesterday or today, as before?"*

¹⁵Then the Israelite foremen went and appealed to Pharaoh: "Why have you treated your servants this way? ¹⁶Your servants are given no straw, yet we are told, 'Make bricks!' Your servants are being beaten, but the fault is with your own people."

¹⁷Pharaoh said, "Lazy, that's what you are—lazy! That is why you keep saying, 'Let us go and sacrifice to the Lord.' ¹⁸Now get to work. You will not be given any straw, yet you must produce your full quota of bricks."

¹⁹The Israelite foremen realized they were in trouble when they were told, "You are not to reduce the number of bricks required of you for each day." ²⁰When they left Pharaoh, they found Moses and Aaron waiting to meet them, ²¹and they said, "May the Lord look upon you and judge you! You have made us a stench to Pharaoh and his officials and have put a sword in their hand to kill us."

²²Moses returned to the Lord and said, "O Lord, why have you brought trouble upon this people? Is this why you sent me? ²³Ever since I went to Pharaoh to speak in your name, he has brought trouble upon this people, and you have not rescued your people at all."

...about today's session

1. What are the three examples mentioned that confirm God is pro-work?

2. What needs does God intend for us to meet from our work's salary?

3. If work is God's design, then why is it often so unfulfilling?

Identifying with the Story

In horseshoe groups of 6–8, explore questions as time allows.

1. What feature of your job makes you feel most like a brick-making Hebrew?

   ☐ my boss
   ☐ my job responsibilities
   ☐ my environment/work conditions
   ☐ other: _____

2. Complete the following sentence: "Something else I identify with in this story is ..."

   ☐ reduced resources and increased expectations.
   ☐ Moses' stress of middle management.
   ☐ declined requests for leave.
   ☐ unjust criticism.
   ☐ company leaders interested only in production, not in the welfare of workers.
   ☐ little or no understanding/acceptance of my spiritual beliefs/practices.
   ☐ other: _____

5

today's session

What is God teaching you from this story?

1. The three main contributors to the stress of work are:

   _____

   _____

   _____

2. What are some ways our actual job responsibilities may invoke stress?

49

3. What are three categories of relationships through which we experience stress in the workplace?

4. What are some of the potential ingredients of stressful working conditions?

Learning from the Story

⊍ **In
horseshoe
groups of 6–8,
choose an
answer and
explain why
you chose
what you did.**

1. On a scale from 1–10, how would you rate your satisfaction with your actual job responsibilities?

   1 · · 2 · · 3 · · 4 · · 5 · · 6 · · 7 · · 8 · · 9 · · 10

very unsatisfied	somewhat unsatisfied	somewhat satisfied	very satisfied

   Which aspect of your job responsibilities is most stressful?

2. Rank in order from "1" (most) to "3" (least) the relationships that create the most stress for you:

   ___ boss(es)
   ___ coworkers
   ___ customers/clients

   From your top-ranked source of relational stress, describe what is so stressful about the relationship.

3. Which of the following conditions or environmental factors cause you stress? Check all that apply.

- ☐ oppressiveness
- ☐ lack of privacy
- ☐ noise
- ☐ monotony
- ☐ isolation
- ☐ chaos
- ☐ office politics
- ☐ constant change
- ☐ danger
- ☐ threat of layoffs
- ☐ other: _____

life change lessons   5

How can you apply this session to your life?

Write your answers here.

1. Identify the _____ _____ of your stress.

2. Determine _____, _____ action steps to reduce the stress.

3. Evaluate your _____ with your job.

Caring Time
15-20 minutes

CARING TIME

♘ Remain in horseshoe groups of 6–8.

Close with a time of prayer for one another. Begin by going around the group and praying for the person on your right. Pray that he or she will be able to determine and follow through on some helpful action steps to reduce the stress of work. Also pray for the concerns and requests listed on the Prayer/Praise Report.

Pray specifically for God to guide you to someone to invite next week to fill the empty chair.

Reference Notes

Use these notes to gain further understanding
of the text as you study on your own.

**EXODUS
5:1**

Afterward Moses and Aaron went to Pharaoh and said. In the previous chapter of Exodus, Moses had been commissioned by God to be His representative before Pharaoh. The hopes of the Israelites were high as they learned that the Lord was concerned for them and had heard their cries for deliverance.

This is what the Lord, the God of Israel, says. This passage begins the confrontation between Moses and Pharaoh. From this point forward until the end of the 12th chapter, God's plan of deliverance unfolds in spite of apparent delays and setbacks.

**EXODUS
5:2**

Who is the Lord, that I should obey him? These are two critical questions that must ultimately be asked and answered by every person. Pharaoh is asking in essence, "Who is this God, and why should I do what He says?" Pharaoh stubbornly refused to acknowledge or respect the authority of the God of Israel. His main concern was for his own "bottom line." He did not want to lose the labor productivity of millions of Israelite workers.

**EXODUS
5:13**

The slave drivers kept pressing them. These slave drivers (taskmasters) were commissioned by Pharaoh and most of the foremen were Israelites! Their duties are described in Exodus 1:11 as being in charge of the Israelite workers to "oppress them with forced labor." The term *slave driver* comes from the Hebrew word *nagas* meaning to drive, harass, tyrannize, or oppress either animals, workers, or debtors. We sometimes use this term today to describe a particularly demanding boss or supervisor.

**EXODUS
5:14**

The Israelite foremen ... were beaten. The Israelite foremen were appointed by the Egyptian slave drivers to supervise the daily work— possibly because they spoke both Hebrew and Egyptian. When faced with the impossible demands of Pharaoh to make bricks without straw, these foremen found themselves being punished for something over which they had no control.

**EXODUS
5:15**

the Israelite foremen ... appealed to Pharaoh. Rather than simply passing the pressure and abuse on down the line to the workers under their authority, the foremen sought to solve the problem at its source. This tendency to cascade the stress down through the ranks of management is a very common problem in our corporate society today. In contrast to this

EXODUS 5:15 (cont'd)	destructive behavior, a godly leader will face his burdens and deal with the real issues at hand rather than trying to force others to meet a set of unrealistic or unfair expectations and requirements.
EXODUS 5:21	***May the Lord look upon you and judge you!*** This is an expression of anger and accusation against Moses and Aaron because the situation had gone from bad to worse.
	stench. This means an abomination or something offensive. Pharaoh now had a reason to further oppress the Hebrews, and the foremen feared for their lives. The people had been expecting a quick deliverance from unfair and harsh labor, but now they faced even more severe challenges.
EXODUS 5:22	***O Lord, why have you brought trouble?*** Even to Moses, it appeared that God's plan had backfired. He then cried out to the Lord for answers and reassurance. In the verses that follow in chapter six, the Lord quickly responded to the doubts and confusion by affirming His redemptive purpose and reminding Moses that a covenant of blood binds God to fulfill His promised deliverance. In like manner, we are bound to God by the covenant of the blood of Jesus Christ. Even when it seems that the situation is out of control, it is never out of God's control. He is working even now behind the scenes to engineer the circumstances we are in for our highest good and His glory.

5

notes

6

The Stress of
Excess Demands

Prepare for the Session

	READINGS	REFLECTIVE QUESTIONS
Monday	Exodus 16:26–30	How difficult is it for you to take a Sabbath rest?
Tuesday	Exodus 18:13–16	When have you felt you were the only one who could do a certain job? How did that affect your stress level?
Wednesday	Exodus 18:17–23	What do you need to delegate so "you will be able to stand the strain"?
Thursday	Exodus 18:24–26	Who could be your Jethro and give you a new perspective on how to organize your day?
Friday	Matthew 11:28–30	How could Jesus' yoke provide you with rest for your soul?
Saturday	Mark 1:32–38	What do you think Jesus prayed about in verse 35? How often does your day start with prayer?
Sunday	Luke 5:15–16	How did Jesus balance the demands of needy people and His need for prayer? How can you follow Jesus' example today?

6

BIBLE STUDY

- to realize the need to seek and protect times of Sabbath rest
- to recognize the overload contributors of excessive responsibility
- to acknowledge the need for and benefit of withdrawal and solitude

LIFE CHANGE

- to mark a weekly Sabbath rest on our calendars and schedule around it
- to list and evaluate the activities we're involved in
- to schedule time alone and time with family and friends

Icebreaker

10-15 minutes

Name Your Race. What kind of race best describes your week?

- ☐ Boston Marathon—My week seemed to last forever.

- ☐ Demolition Derby—I feel beat up.

- ☐ Tour de France—I was peddling uphill as fast as I could.

- ☐ Kentucky Derby—I worked for so long on something that was over so quickly.

- ☐ Indy 500—I went 'round and 'round and I'm right where I started.

- ☐ Ironman Triathlon—I had a week full of job, family, and church activities.

- ☐ 24 Hours of LeMans—Sleep? What's that?

- ☐ Hundred-Meter High Hurdles—I had to sprint and deal with obstacles almost every step of the way.

- ☐ Other:_____

Information to Remember: In the spaces provided, take note of information you will need as you participate in this group in the weeks to come.

PEOPLE:

1. A person in the group I would like to hear more from today is:

2. A person in this group who has really been a blessing to me during these sessions is:

EVENTS: An event that is coming up that I want to make sure I am part of is _____. It will be _____ (time) on _____ (date) at _____ (location).

And if I have time, I would also like to be part of _____. It will be _____ (time) on _____ (date) at _____ (location).

Bible Study

30-45 minutes

The Scripture for this week:

¹³*The next day Moses took his seat to serve as judge for the people, and they stood around him from morning till evening.* ¹⁴*When his father-in-law saw all that Moses was doing for the people, he said, "What is this you are doing for the people? Why do you alone sit as judge, while all these people stand around you from morning till evening?"*

¹⁵*Moses answered him, "Because the people come to me to seek God's will.* ¹⁶*Whenever they have a dispute, it is brought to me, and I decide between the parties and inform them of God's decrees and laws."*

¹⁷*Moses' father-in-law replied, "What you are doing is not good.* ¹⁸*You and these people who come to you will only wear yourselves out. The work is too heavy for you; you cannot handle it alone.* ¹⁹*Listen now to me and I will give you some advice, and may God be with*

you. You must be the people's representative before God and bring their disputes to him. [20]Teach them the decrees and laws, and show them the way to live and the duties they are to perform. [21]But select capable men from all the people—men who fear God, trustworthy men who hate dishonest gain—and appoint them as officials over thousands, hundreds, fifties and tens. [22]Have them serve as judges for the people at all times, but have them bring every difficult case to you; the simple cases they can decide themselves. That will make your load lighter, because they will share it with you. [23]If you do this and God so commands, you will be able to stand the strain, and all these people will go home satisfied."

[24]Moses listened to his father-in-law and did everything he said. [25]He chose capable men from all Israel and made them leaders of the people, officials over thousands, hundreds, fifties and tens. [26]They served as judges for the people at all times. The difficult cases they brought to Moses, but the simple ones they decided themselves.

...about today's session

**A WORD
FROM THE
LEADER**

**Write your
answers
here.**

1. What is a "margin"?

2. How does the concept of "margins" apply to our experience of overload?

3. What is the result of ignoring the need for margins in our lives?

Identifying with the Story

◡ In
horseshoe
groups
of 6–8,
explore
questions as
time allows.

1. In what area(s) do you feel most overloaded with responsibilities?

   ☐ immediate family   ☐ church
   ☐ career/work   ☐ civic/community involvement
   ☐ extended family   ☐ other:_____

2. Besides yourself, who else is affected by the stress of your overload?

   ☐ spouse   ☐ friends
   ☐ children   ☐ coworkers
   ☐ other family members   ☐ clients/customers
   ☐ other:_____

3. Which statement below best describes your feeling of overload?

   ☐ I'm swimming as fast as I can ... in quicksand.
   ☐ I feel like a giant ice cream soda and everyone has a straw.
   ☐ What I need is a life preserver, but my boss just threw me the anchor.
   ☐ My ship is sinking, and I can't figure out what to throw overboard.
   ☐ Not only am I stuck on the merry-go-round, it's speeding up.
   ☐ I need eight arms like an octopus and the energy of a sugar-spiked four-year-old.

6

today's session

What is God
teaching you
from this
story?

1. How did the early Hebrews ignore God's provision of the Sabbath?

2. How does observing a Sabbath provide healthy margins to your life?

3. What are some of the reasons we take on or keep too much responsibility?

4. In what way was Moses encouraged to install margins to treat the stress of his overload?

5. How did Jesus create margins in the midst of a demanding ministry?

Learning from the Story

♘ **In
horseshoe
groups of 6–8,
choose an
answer and
explain why
you chose
what you did.**

1. Do you guard a "Sabbath" day during the week? How restful or re-energizing is your "Sabbath"?

2. Which of the four contributing factors to overload causes you to take on too much?

   ☐ I think an opportunity looks good at the time and it's something I'd enjoy, but I don't consider the time it will take.
   ☐ I can't seem to say no without feeling guilty.
   ☐ I am a perfectionist who wants things done right so I do them myself.
   ☐ I need to feel needed and irreplaceable.

3. What should we learn from Jesus' regular use of the margin of solitude? If seeking solitude was a consistent practice of Christ, why do you suppose we consider it optional?

life change lessons

How can you apply this session to your life?

Write your answers here.

1. What does "practicing Sabbath" not mean? Specifically and practically, how will you create a Sabbath?

2. What activities do you need to eliminate or get help with?

6

3. What are some important things to keep in mind when asking others to help you in your management of responsibilities?

4. What practical and even creative steps can you take to install the margins of withdrawal and solitude?

Caring Time

15-20 minutes

CARING TIME

♥ **Remain in horseshoe groups of 6–8.**

During this time of prayer, ask God to help each group member have wisdom and discernment in determining how to properly balance work and rest, thereby decreasing stress due to overload. Remember to include prayer for the concerns listed on the Prayer/Praise Report.

Pray specifically for God to guide you to someone to invite next week to fill the empty chair.

Conclude your prayer time by reading together the words of Jesus in Matthew 11:28–30:

"Come to me, all you who are weary and burdened, and I will give you rest. Take my yoke upon you and learn from me, for I am gentle and humble in heart, and you will find rest for your souls. For my yoke is easy and my burden is light."

Reference Notes

BIBLE STUDY NOTES

Use these notes to gain further understanding
of the text as you study on your own.

EXODUS 18:13

took his seat to serve as judge. Moses is introduced in the role of judge. In addition to being a prophet, deliverer, mediator, moral, spiritual, and military leader, Moses is also a judge.

EXODUS 18:16

dispute. The Hebrew word is *dabar*, which does not necessarily mean conflicting arguments or cases. It can mean any matter needing clarification or settlement. Certainly, more serious and volatile issues were brought to Moses as well. In the previous verse, when Moses declares that the people come to him to seek God's will, there is an implied connection to disputes. The people came to Moses to have him evaluate and respond to their questions, concerns, debates, and offenses on the basis of his knowledge of God's will and ways ("inform them of God's decrees and laws"). In a sense, Moses was operating as a counselor and as a judge.

EXODUS 18:19 *You must be the people's representative before God.* Moses' father-in-law acknowledges that there are some duties that only Moses is qualified to do.

EXODUS 18:21 *select capable men.* Being capable is the first of four qualifications required of the men who would share judicial responsibility. Capable (*chayil*) often means physical strength, so these men must be in good health since stamina would be needed in this role. Secondly, these deputized judges must fear God and be men who demonstrate genuine reverence and devotion to God. Thirdly, these men must be trustworthy, faithful, reliable, and dependable. Lastly, these men must hate dishonest gain; they must abhor and refuse bribes.

appoint them as officials over thousands, hundreds, fifties and tens. Jethro proposed an organizational structure to handle the matters efficiently but retained higher levels of authority to whom to appeal.

EXODUS 18:22 *have them bring every difficult case to you.* Moses' exceptional knowledge and wisdom would be sought in complex cases where the appointed judges felt unqualified to render a decision.

EXODUS 18:24 *Moses listened to his father-in-law.* Moses' greatness as a leader is seen in his humility as a leader, here willing to consider a different method of leadership.

6

notes

The Stress of Crisis

Prepare for the Session

	READINGS	REFLECTIVE QUESTIONS
Monday	Luke 13:1–3	When have you asked why something bad happened to you or someone else?
Tuesday	Luke 13:4–5	What is Jesus saying here about the most important concern we should have in life?
Wednesday	1 Peter 4:12–19	When have you suffered for being a Christian? What was your response?
Thursday	James 1:2–4	How has suffering in your life caused you to be more "mature and complete"?
Friday	2 Corinthians 4:7–9	Where do you need God's "all-surpassing power" in your life today?
Saturday	Psalm 34:18; 147:3	What is God's response to us when we suffer? How can you pass this compassion on to someone else?
Sunday	Romans 8:18,22–25	What hope do you cling to in the midst of suffering?

BIBLE STUDY
- to recognize our drive to solve the mystery of suffering
- to understand the distinction between affliction and evil
- to consider how our attitude about suffering may actually prolong our suffering

LIFE CHANGE
- to accept the reality of problems
- to draw support from others in times of crisis
- to offer support to others in times of crisis

lcebreaker

10-15 minutes

GATHERING THE PEOPLE ⊍ Form horseshoe groups of 6–8.

This Week's Journey. Imagine this past week was a trail that goes along a mountain range. Take turns answering question 1; then go around again on question 2, etc.

1. When did the "trail" seem so steep you wished you could turn around and go back?

2. What beauty did you experience that made it, at least for the moment, seem all worthwhile?

3. Who did you meet along the trail who made the "hike" more enjoyable?

Information to Remember: Finish the following sentences as you look around at the people here today.

1. A person who looks like he or she could use some extra loving care is:

2. A person I really wish I could get to know better is:

Bible Study
30-45 minutes

The Scripture for this week:

LEARNING FROM THE BIBLE

LUKE 13:1–5

¹Now there were some present at that time who told Jesus about the Galileans whose blood Pilate had mixed with their sacrifices. ²Jesus answered, "Do you think that these Galileans were worse sinners than all the other Galileans because they suffered this way? ³I tell you, no! But unless you repent, you too will all perish. ⁴Or those eighteen who died when the tower in Siloam fell on them—do you think they were more guilty than all the others living in Jerusalem? ⁵I tell you, no! But unless you repent, you too will all perish."

...about today's session

A WORD FROM THE LEADER

Write your answers here.

1. In reacting to suffering, what are some wrong conclusions one might draw concerning God?

2. How is suffering like a tornado?

Identifying with the Story

In horseshoe groups of 6–8, explore questions as time allows.

1. What is the most difficult or tragic life experience you have ever faced?

2. Which of the following responses did you have to that situation?

   ☐ God does not exist.
   ☐ God must be testing me.
   ☐ God must be trying to teach me a lesson.
   ☐ God's presence is giving me strength.
   ☐ God does not care.
   ☐ God must be punishing me for something.
   ☐ God isn't powerful enough.
   ☐ God is absent.
   ☐ God is silent.
   ☐ Other: _____

today's session

What is God teaching you from this story?

1. What is the natural and basic question we ask in the midst of crisis?

2. How did the people of Jesus' day resolve the dilemma about why bad things happen to good people?

3. What are the two tragic events described in today's passage?

   _____

   _____

68

4. What two dynamics of human suffering does the Scripture passage illustrate?

_____

_____

5. According to the session, our suffering will likely be prolonged and joy in our lives will be elusive if we:

1. Expect _____ from suffering.

2. Demand to know _____ the suffering occurred.

3. Require that the suffering be promptly _____.

Learning from the Story

In horseshoe groups of 6–8, choose an answer and explain why you chose what you did.

1. What is the problem with a relentless pursuit of asking "why?"

2. What is the difference between affliction and evil? In what way have you experienced each?

3. Which of these three subtle expectations do you most likely have?
   ☐ I expect immunity from suffering.
   ☐ I demand to know why the suffering occurred.
   ☐ I require that the suffering be promptly alleviated.

7

life change lessons

1. What happens when our expectation is for God to prevent or end our suffering?

2. What gift has God given us for support during times of crisis?

3. How is it beneficial to you when you are suffering to help someone else who is suffering?

Caring Time

15-20 minutes

CARING TIME

♆ **Remain in horseshoe groups of 6–8.**

Is anyone in your group going through a time of crisis or suffering? Offer your support through prayer and encouragement. Also, use the Prayer/Praise Report that your leader gives you and pray for the requests and concerns listed.

Pray specifically for God to guide you to someone to invite next week to fill the empty chair.

BIBLE STUDY NOTES

Reference Notes

Use these notes to gain further understanding
of the text as you study on your own.

Starting in Luke 12:54, Jesus turns His attention from His disciples and begins to speak directly to the crowd that had been following Him. He teaches them several important truths about life, one of which is the focus of our text. In this section, Jesus taught the multitudes that calamity can come into any life at any moment. He used two examples to illustrate the fact that no one is immune to crisis.

LUKE 13:1

Galileans whose blood. This incident is not described or explained elsewhere, but it was common in the days of Pilate for the Jewish people to experience persecution, even as they worshiped God.

LUKE 13:2

worse sinners. In ancient as well as modern times, it has often been assumed that "bad" things should not happen to "good" people. In John 9:1–2, we find this way of thinking prevalent in the attitude of Jesus' disciples toward a blind man. They assumed that either the man himself or his parents must have sinned to cause his condition. In Job 4:7, Job's friend Eliphaz falsely accused him of creating his own troubles as a result of living a disobedient life before God. The crowd surrounding Jesus in this text mistakenly believed that sudden death was reserved only for those who were the worst sinners.

LUKE 13:4

more guilty. The second example of calamity or crisis concerned 18 seemingly innocent and undeserving victims who were killed when the tower of Siloam, located in Jerusalem, fell on them. In the first example of the Galileans, religious persecution could at least be considered an explanation for the devastation. In the tower example, however, disaster simply strikes—without warning or reason.

LUKE 13:3,5

I tell you, no! Jesus is making the point that neither life nor death, calamity nor prosperity, is a measure of a person's righteousness. Anyone can find himself or herself in crisis. While it is true that sin can and does often bring about devastating consequences (Num. 32:23; Ps. 32:3–5), it is not true that difficulties and troubles are always the direct result of personal sin.

unless you repent, you too will all perish. Trouble or even death can knock on our door at any time. Only God's grace can usher us into His kingdom, and only repentance can open the access to His grace. The word for repentance is *metanoeo*, meaning to reconsider or perceive and think differently. It reflects a change of mind and heart. The Lord offers each of us the assurance that no matter what happens, He is faithful to those who trust Him. Romans 8:35–39 encourages us with the confidence that no crisis, including death itself, can ever "separate us from the love of God that is in Christ Jesus our Lord (v. 39)."

notes

Session

8

The Stress of Anger

Prepare for the Session

	READINGS	REFLECTIVE QUESTIONS
Monday	Ephesians 4:25–26	When have you said something in anger that you regretted?
Tuesday	Ephesians 4:26–27	How often do you "let the sun go down while you are still angry"? How does unresolved anger give the devil a foothold?
Wednesday	Ephesians 4:28–29	Who could you build up today with some encouraging words?
Thursday	Ephesians 4:30–32	Which command in these verses is most challenging for you?
Friday	Proverbs 29:11	What helps you keep your anger under control?
Saturday	Mark 3:1–5	What kind of anger is not sinful?
Sunday	James 1:19–20	Pray that today you can be "quick to listen, slow to speak and slow to become angry."

8

BIBLE STUDY
- to understand the underlying roots of anger
- to recognize unhealthy/ungodly expressions of anger
- to identify healthy/godly expressions of anger

LIFE CHANGE
- to admit to ourselves and to God that we are angry
- to restrain our immediate anger response and locate the root of our anger
- to identify the goal of our anger and proceed with gentleness

Icebreaker

10-15 minutes

**GATHERING
THE PEOPLE
U Form
horseshoe
groups of 6–8.**

Anger Profile. Go around the group and take turns completing the first statement. Then go around again and complete the second statement.

1. When I'm angry, other people probably experience me as:

   ☐ cold (as in giving them the cold shoulder)
   ☐ warm (as in I'm pretending to be just fine)
   ☐ simmering (as in I'm hot but under control)
   ☐ boiling (as in I'm ready to explode)

2. When someone is angry at me I'm a:

   ☐ boomerang—here's the anger back at ya, pal
   ☐ sponge—the anger is absorbed and disappears
   ☐ piston—too much friction and I just shut down
   ☐ baseball glove—catch the anger and hold it
   ☐ fish hook—if you bite me you'll wish you hadn't
   ☐ bulletproof vest—the anger doesn't phase me
   ☐ sand castle—anger flattens me like a wave
   ☐ other:_____

Information to Remember: In the spaces provided, take note of information you will need as you participate in this group in the weeks to come.

PEOPLE:

1. Someone normally here who is missing this week is:

2. What I can do to help this person know he or she was missed is:

EVENTS: An event that is coming up that I want to make sure I am part of is _____. It will be _____ (time) on _____ (date) at _____ (location).

And if I have time, I would also like to be part of _____. It will be _____ (time) on _____ (date) at _____ (location).

Bible Study

30-45 minutes

The Scripture for this week:

²⁵*Therefore each of you must put off falsehood and speak truthfully to his neighbor, for we are all members of one body.* ²⁶*"In your anger do not sin": Do not let the sun go down while you are still angry,* ²⁷*and do not give the devil a foothold.* ²⁸*He who has been stealing must steal no longer, but must work, doing something useful with his own hands, that he may have something to share with those in need.*

²⁹*Do not let any unwholesome talk come out of your mouths, but only what is helpful for building others up according to their needs, that it may benefit those who listen.* ³⁰*And do not grieve the Holy Spirit of God, with whom you were sealed for the day of redemption.* ³¹*Get rid of all bitterness, rage and anger, brawling and slander, along with every form of malice.* ³²*Be kind and compassionate to one another, forgiving each other, just as in Christ God forgave you.*

8

...about today's session

1. Why is anger not inherently or automatically sinful?

2. What damage can inappropriate anger cause?

Identifying with the Story

 In horseshoe groups of 6–8, explore questions as time allows.

1. Do you seek to throw out anger like soured milk, or do you preserve it over time as though it were wine?

2. Complete the following sentence: "The way I deal with anger in the amount of territory I unwittingly give to the devil is probably comparable to the size of …"

   - ☐ a postage stamp
   - ☐ my front yard
   - ☐ Central Park
   - ☐ my garage
   - ☐ a football field
   - ☐ Texas

3. Who did you feel mad at this past week?

   - ☐ my boss
   - ☐ a coworker
   - ☐ myself
   - ☐ a friend
   - ☐ another driver
   - ☐ a store clerk
   - ☐ a family member
   - ☐ a church member
   - ☐ God
   - ☐ other:_____

today's session

What is God teaching you from this story?

1. Why is anger not a "primary" emotion? What is the main underlying feeling that gives rise to anger?

2. What are the two main unhealthy/ungodly ways of expressing anger?

3. What are the potential consequences of allowing "the sun to go down on your anger"?

4. What are some of the verbal manifestations of explosive anger?

5. Anger always has two elements:

Constructive anger pursues a resolution of the _____ issue and preserves or rebuilds a bridge for the

Learning from the Story

♉ In horseshoe groups of 6–8, choose an answer and explain why you chose what you did.

1. Which is most true of your style of managing anger?

   ☐ I hold it in. (implosive)
   ☐ I let it fly. (explosive)
   ☐ I express it appropriately. (constructive)

2. If anger is a response to perceived injustice, which of the following "wrongs" sparked a recent feeling of anger for you?

   ☐ insulted   ☐ mocked   ☐ unappreciated
   ☐ manipulated   ☐ betrayed   ☐ disrespected
   ☐ ignored   ☐ threatened   ☐ accused
   ☐ humiliated   ☐ other:_____

3. If the godly goals of anger are to resolve the content problem and preserve/restore the relationship, what percentage of the time does your anger conclude with those goals met?

   ☐ 0 percent   ☐ 40 percent   ☐ 80 percent
   ☐ 20 percent   ☐ 60 percent   ☐ 100 percent

8

life change lessons

How can you apply this session to your life?

Write your answers here.

1. Admit to _____ and to _____ that you are angry.

2. _____ your immediate anger response and locate the _____ of your anger.

3. Identify the _____ of your anger and proceed with _____.

Caring Time

15-20 minutes

Take this time to encourage one another in prayer. Ask for God's help to express anger in a healthy and productive way. Pray, also, for the concerns and requests listed on the Prayer/Praise Report.

Pray specifically for God to guide you to someone to invite next week to fill the empty chair.

Reference Notes

Use these notes to gain further understanding
of the text as you study on your own.

Beginning in verse 1 of chapter 4, Paul exhorts believers to "live a life worthy of the calling you have received." He speaks of "putting off your old self" and "putting on the new self." Because of what God has done for us, both in sacrificing His own Son on our behalf and then sending His Spirit to live within us, we are able to live new lives. In the section before us, Paul presents five major exhortations to the high calling of following Christ.

A common three-part pattern is repeated in each of the exhortations. There is a (1) negative command; (2) a positive command; and (3) a reason or motivation for putting off the old and putting on the new.

put off falsehood and speak truthfully. The negative command is to put off or to put away falsehood (*pseudos*, meaning lying or deceitfulness). The positive command is to speak truthfully. Earlier in this same chapter, Paul also encourages his readers to not only speak the truth, but to speak "the truth in love" (4:15). The reason Paul gives in verse 25 for putting away the false and speaking only the truth is that we are all members of one body.

In your anger do not sin. Some anger is sinful; some is not. Jesus displayed righteous anger as He purified the temple of sinful practices (Matt. 21:12–13). Paul exhorts us to guard against allowing anger to manifest itself in sinful thoughts or practices. The key is to deal with anger swiftly and decisively (before the sun goes down). The reason for taking such prompt measures is to prevent the devil from gaining a foothold (*topos*, meaning a place or an opportunity).

EPHESIANS **4:28**	***steal no longer ... share with those in need.*** Paul exhorts believers to stop taking from others (stealing) and start giving to others (sharing). The phrase "doing something useful" comes from the Greek word *agathon*, meaning good or beneficial. The motivation is that of ministering to those in need. God has established daily work as a means of providing for our own personal needs, giving us a sense of purpose and accomplishment, and enabling us to help others by sharing material possessions.
EPHESIANS **4:29**	***helpful ... building others up ... benefit.*** Believers are to guard against unwholesome words (*sapros*, meaning rotten). Instead, we should sift our words through a three-point purity test: (1) Are my words helpful? (2) Do they build someone up according to their needs? (3) Are they beneficial to the listener?
EPHESIANS **4:30**	***do not grieve the Holy Spirit.*** As we yield our lives to the Holy Spirit (Gal. 5:16), He helps us guard our words, thoughts, and actions. The word for *grieve* is *lupe*, meaning to be sad or sorrowful. The fact that we can grieve the Holy Spirit demonstrates the reality that He is a person, capable of experiencing emotion. We are reminded that the Holy Spirit not only resides within believers but that His presence is a seal until the day of redemption when believers will receive their new and glorified bodies (Eph. 1:13-14; Phil. 3:20–21).
EPHESIANS **4:31–32**	***Get rid of ... just as in Christ.*** In this final exhortation, Paul highlights six additional elements of our sinful nature that are to be laid aside and three characteristics of our new life in Christ to be "put on" in daily practice. The sinful attitudes and practices to be rid of (*apotithemi*, meaning cast off) include bitterness, rage (*thumos*, meaning fierce anger), anger (*orge*, indicating a settled anger with a view toward revenge), brawling (*krauge*, depicting verbal barrage or outcry), slander (*blasphemia*) and malice (*kakia*, meaning vicious character). The positive attributes are kindness (*chrestoi*, gracious action toward another person), compassion (*eusplanchnoi*, meaning good-hearted), and forgiveness (*charizomai*, to bestow a favor unconditionally). The reason behind the exhortation is that God has already bestowed His forgiveness, compassion, and kindness upon us beyond measure. As illustrated in the parable of the unmerciful servant (Matt. 18:21–35), we have been forgiven a debt of sin that we can never repay. We then should reflect toward others what we have so graciously received from God.

8

notes

The Stress of Negative Evaluation

Prepare for the Session

	READINGS	REFLECTIVE QUESTIONS
Monday	1 Corinthians 4:1–4	How does your usual reaction to criticism compare to Paul's commands in these verses?
Tuesday	1 Corinthians 4:5	In what situations do you tend to judge others?
Wednesday	Matthew 9:9–13	How do you feel when you are criticized for doing something good?
Thursday	Matthew 12:9–13	What is the implied criticism of Jesus here? How does Jesus respond?
Friday	Galatians 1:6–10	In what recent situations have you been more concerned about pleasing people than pleasing God?
Saturday	Galatians 2:11–16	What was Paul's motive in criticizing Peter?
Sunday	1 Peter 2:21–23	How can you follow Jesus' example in the face of criticism?

9

BIBLE STUDY
- to recognize our three critics as revealed by Paul
- to identify our personal targets of criticism
- to consider Paul's response to criticism

LIFE CHANGE
- to recognize that critics are not necessarily enemies
- to assess the critic's credibility
- to analyze constructive criticism for validity

Icebreaker

10-15 minutes

The Winner's Circle. In what "Olympic Event" did you win a medal (bronze, silver, or gold) recently?

☐ The Week with Kids Decathlon—We have so many activities, programs, and places to be.

☐ Temptation Hurdles—I said no!

☐ Sick Baby Marathon—I'm exhausted.

☐ Boxing with the Boss—Well, at least in my mind we went a couple of rounds.

☐ Greco-Roman Wrestling with Teenagers—If I won, why do I feel so sore?

☐ Diplomacy Balance Beam—I had to step carefully regarding an issue.

☐ Office Synchronized Swimming—At my workplace I'd call it drowning with style.

☐ Burden Weightlifting—I have a friend I'm worried about.

☐ Church Leader Triathlon—I had events at home, work, and church.

Information to Remember: In the spaces provided, take note of information you will need as you participate in this group in the weeks to come.

PEOPLE:

1. A person here I would like to hear more from today is:

2. A person here to whom God may be leading me to say something special today is:

EVENTS: An event that is coming up that I want to make sure I am part of is _____. It will be _____ (time) on _____ (date) at _____ (location).

And if I have time, I would also like to be part of _____. It will be _____ (time) on _____ (date) at _____ (location).

Bible Study

30-45 minutes

The Scripture for this week:

LEARNING FROM THE BIBLE

CORINTHIANS 4:1-5

[1]Men ought to regard us as servants of Christ and as those entrusted with the secret things of God. [2]Now it is required that those who have been given a trust must prove faithful. [3]I care very little if I am judged by you or by any human court; indeed, I do not even judge myself. [4]My conscience is clear, but that does not make me innocent. It is the Lord who judges me. [5]Therefore, judge nothing before the appointed time; wait till the Lord comes. He will bring to light what is hidden in darkness and will expose the motives of men's hearts. At that time each will receive his praise from God.

1. Name two examples of outstanding men who remind us that displaying pure motives, sacrifice, goodness, and even holiness will not shield one from criticism.

Identifying with the Story

1. My most recent dose of criticism came from:

☐ my boss   ☐ a coworker   ☐ a leader
☐ my parent(s)   ☐ a friend   ☐ a teacher
☐ a church member ☐ my spouse   ☐ other:_____
☐ a customer/client ☐ a member of a committee/group
☐ a family member ☐ someone who barely knows me

2. I felt the criticism was:

☐ unfounded   ☐ done in love   ☐ unfair
☐ partially true   ☐ constructive   ☐ harsh
☐ unsolicited   ☐ justified   ☐ other:_____
☐ instructive   ☐ balanced with encouragement

3. My response to criticism is usually:

☐ feeling defeated   ☐ pretending that I can handle it
☐ defending myself   ☐ analyzing it for truth
☐ criticizing the critic ☐ trying to win back approval
☐ silent anger   ☐ other:_____

What is God teaching you from this story?

1. Who are our three ever-present critics?

2. What are the three primary personal targets of criticism?

   _____

   _____

   _____

3. What are some secondary lightning rods for criticism?

4. What are some of the issues to consider when asking yourself, "Do I respect the critic?"

5. What are some suggestions made by Backus and Chapin about responding to angry, destructive criticism?

9

6. What does Paul think about his ability to judge himself?

7. Where can we take refuge against the painful and perhaps unrelenting criticism of others?

Learning from the Story

⊍ In horseshoe groups of 6–8, choose an answer and explain why you chose what you did.

1. In what area have you recently received criticism? Place a ✔ in the box. In what area are you most sensitive? Place an **X** in the box.

   ☐ character   ☐ competence
   ☐ relationships   ☐ personal appearance
   ☐ personality   ☐ ideas, beliefs, or opinions
   ☐ other:_____

2. In today's session, we learned that we have three judges. Who do you think is your harshest critic?

   ☐ others   ☐ myself   ☐ God

3. When evaluating criticism from another person, why is the question, "Do I respect the critic?" so important to answer?

4. Why is your own conscience an unreliable judge?

5. How is the truth that God is the all-knowing and final Judge both reassuring and disturbing?

life change lessons

How can you apply this session to your life?

Write your answers here.

1. Recognize that critics are not necessarily _____.
   According to John Ortberg, what kind of addiction makes us hypersensitive to criticism?

2. First, you must assume that you have _____ and need help seeing them. Second, you must make a commitment to be

_____.

3. Assess the critic's _____. What are some factors that lessen the validity of a critic's comments?

4. Analyze constructive criticism for _____. What should you look for in the analysis?

Caring Time

15-20 minutes

CARING TIME

♆ **Remain in horseshoe groups of 6–8.**

Have group members pray for the person on their right. Pray that he or she will see criticism as an opportunity for growth, and at the same time remember how much Jesus loves him or her. Begin by completing this sentence:

"Dear God, I want to speak to you about my friend _____."

Also remember to pray for the concerns listed on the Prayer/Praise Report.

Pray specifically for God to guide you to someone to invite next week to fill the empty chair.

9

Reference Notes

Use these notes to gain further understanding
of the text as you study on your own.

Throughout the previous chapter, Paul has been addressing one specific cause of division in the Corinthian church—a misunderstanding of both ministry and ministers. The Corinthians had been focusing their attention on men rather than on God alone, the source of all blessing. Ministers, as Paul points out, are merely servants accountable to God for the tasks He assigns them to accomplish.

**I CORINTHIANS
4:1**

Men ought to regard us as servants of Christ. The word used here for servant is *huperetes*, meaning a subordinate acting under another's direction. It was used to describe one who served as a rower on a ship.

entrusted with the secret things of God. The word for secret is *musterion* from which we get the word mystery. It denotes things beyond human understanding made known only by divine revelation at a time appointed by God to those filled by the Holy Spirit (1 Cor. 2:9–14).

**I CORINTHIANS
4:2**

must prove faithful. The Greek word for faithful, *pistos*, denotes reliability and trustworthiness. Paul's desire was that the ministers of the gospel would proclaim the message accurately and faithfully for their Lord, rather than being concerned with the opinions or judgments of men.

**I CORINTHIANS
4:3**

I care very little. This phrase can also be translated, "I consider it a very small thing." The word is *elachistos*, meaning something of the least importance or significance. Rather than allowing his actions or words to be dictated by a desire for the approval of men, Paul's heart was set upon pleasing his Master and Lord.

judged by you ... not even judge myself. Paul says he is not concerned about being judged by others (*anakrino*, meaning scrutinized, investigated, examined, or searched). He is not even capable of accurately judging or discerning his own motives, nor the level of faithfulness to his Lord's service.

**I CORINTHIANS
4:4**

conscience is clear ... It is the Lord who judges. Only God is fully qualified to judge. The word used to indicate God's judgment is *krino*, meaning to decide, to determine, or to pass sentence. Neither the opinions of others nor our own judgment or conscience is a reliable and unbiased standard of accountability.

**I CORINTHIANS
4:5**

appointed time. Paul exhorts his readers to guard against premature judgment because it leads to either the exaltation or the condemnation of others, both of which are harmful extremes. At the appointed time

(1 Cor. 3:13), God will judge believers, and the quality of each person's work on earth will be tested to determine its eternal value.

bring to light ... expose the motives. In Hebrews 4:12–13, God's Word is described as a sharp and penetrating two-edged sword, capable of judging the "thoughts and attitudes of the heart." It continues with the sobering twin truths that (1) "Nothing ... is hidden"; and (2) "Everything is uncovered" before the eyes of God. At the final divine judgment all of the facts will be clear, and God will administer His praise to those whose hearts have been faithful. All of the unfair and undeserved criticism of people will fade from view in the light of the glorious words of our Lord to all whose hearts sought to serve Him, "Well done, good and faithful servant!" (Matt. 25:21).

9

notes

The Stress of Change

Prepare for the Session

	READINGS	REFLECTIVE QUESTIONS
Monday	Genesis 12:1–5	How would you respond if God told you to leave your country?
Tuesday	Exodus 3:1–12	When have you felt that God was asking you to do the impossible?
Wednesday	Philippians 2:6–8	What changes did Jesus go through to become the One who saved you from eternal death?
Thursday	1 Corinthians 15:51–54	Which of these changes are you most looking forward to?
Friday	Luke 1:26–38	How did Mary respond to the announcement that her life was about to change radically?
Saturday	Hebrews 13:8	How does this verse comfort you in a rapidly changing world?
Sunday	Philippians 4:13	In what ways do you need God's strength today to cope with the stress of changes in your life?

10

BIBLE STUDY
- to recognize the four quadrants of change and the many arenas of change
- to identify reasons for our resistance to change and the three questions raised by change
- to realize that change carries the potential to produce personal growth, as seen in the lives of Abram and other biblical figures

LIFE CHANGE
- to anticipate change without becoming a pessimist
- to accept change without becoming bitter
- to cling to God during times of change

Icebreaker

10-15 minutes

My, How You've Changed. From the following list, select two items to describe from your teen years.

- ✧ My favorite musical group
- ✧ Something I wore that is sorely out of fashion now
- ✧ My hairstyle
- ✧ One of my favorite leisure activities
- ✧ My favorite reading material
- ✧ A boyfriend/girlfriend
- ✧ A bad habit
- ✧ My treatment of my parents
- ✧ A best friend
- ✧ How my bedroom was decorated

Information to Remember: Finish the following sentences as you look around at the people here today.

1. Someone normally here who is missing this week is:

2. What I could do to help this person know that he or she was missed is:

Bible Study

30-45 minutes

The Scripture for this week:

¹The Lord had said to Abram, "Leave your country, your people and your father's household and go to the land I will show you.
²"I will make you into a great nation
    and I will bless you;
I will make your name great,
    and you will be a blessing.
³I will bless those who bless you,
    and whoever curses you I will curse;
and all peoples on earth
    will be blessed through you."
⁴So Abram left, as the Lord had told him; and Lot went with him. Abram was seventy-five years old when he set out from Haran. ⁵He took his wife Sarai, his nephew Lot, all the possessions they had accumulated and the people they had acquired in Haran, and they set out for the land of Canaan, and they arrived there.

...about today's session

**A WORD
FROM THE
LEADER**

1. What invention has sparked unprecedented change in our lifetime?

**Write your
answers
here.**

2. Does the stress of changes we experience come primarily as a result of global factors or is it due to more personal issues?

10

3. What are the four ways we experience change in our lives?

1. _____ and _____

2. _____ and _____

3. _____ and _____

4. _____ and _____

4. Which typifies the most stressful change?

Identifying with the Story

In
horseshoe
groups
of 6–8,
explore
questions as
time allows.

1. If you were required to relocate to another city, what or who would you miss the most about your present community? (Rank in order your top 3.)

___ family   ___ climate   ___ job
___ my child's school   ___ house   ___ church
___ favorite restaurants ___ friends   ___ other:_____
___ neighborhood   ___ recreation/cultural activities

2. What or who would you miss the least?

☐ job   ☐ commute   ☐ boss
☐ cost of living   ☐ dentist   ☐ traffic
☐ school system   ☐ landlord   ☐ house
☐ neighborhood   ☐ climate   ☐ other:_____

3. In what quadrant have you most recently experienced change?

☐ expected and welcome   ☐ expected and unwelcome
☐ unexpected and welcome   ☐ unexpected and unwelcome

4. Your company has told you that they have an *incredible* new opportunity for you in another city. They won't tell you where it is, and you must put your house up for sale and load up the moving van before you receive an envelope with directions to your new home. How would you respond to their offer?

today's session

What is God teaching you from this story?

1. What are some of the arenas where we experience change?

2. What are some of the reasons we resist change?

3. In what way was Abram's move unsettling?

4. Not only does change bring a sense of _____, it veils the _____ in mystery.

5. What are two positive things that change potentially promotes?

Learning from the Story

In horseshoe groups of 6–8, choose an answer and explain why you chose that you did.

1. The arena of life in which I've experienced the most change recently is:

   ☐ life cycle change   ☐ vocational change
   ☐ relationship change   ☐ health change
   ☐ cultural change   ☐ financial change
   ☐ residential change   ☐ other:_____

2. Who are some biblical characters cited in the session (and some who were not cited), who were either called upon or forced to adapt to change? Who do you most identify with?

10

3. What do we typically consider to be the negative aspects of change? How can God strategically use change in your life?

life change lessons

How can you apply this session to your life?

Write your answers here.

1. Anticipate change without becoming a _____. What is something you can look for in your daily Bible reading?

2. Accept change without becoming _____. What are two recommended passages in Philippians to memorize?

3. Cling to _____ during times of _____. What are two images of your soul clinging to God?

Caring Time

15-20 minutes

CARING TIME

◡ Remain in horseshoe groups of 6–8.

Close by praying for one another. Have each person in the group share the arena of life in which he or she has experienced the most change recently (as expressed in answer to question 1 under "Learning from the Story"). Pray that God will provide wisdom, strength, and hope in each situation. In addition, pray for the concerns and requests listed on the Prayer/Praise Report.

Pray specifically for God to guide you to someone to invite next week to fill the empty chair.

Reference Notes

BIBLE STUDY NOTES

Use these notes to gain further understanding
of the text as you study on your own.

The book of Genesis changes direction and focus in the first verse of chapter 12. Up to that point, God's plan and purpose for all creation was in view. The development of humankind, the fall to sin, the judgment of the flood, and the rebuilding of the human race are all described in the first 11 chapters of Genesis. Beginning in chapter 12, the focus shifts to one man, Abram (later to be called Abraham), and God's specific plan for his life. The Lord calls Abram to take a step of incredible faith, and through the obedience of one man, God unfolds His marvelous redemption of all mankind.

GENESIS 12:1

The Lord had said. Genesis 11 recounts the narrative of Abram's family history as they journeyed from the land of Ur to Canaan, with a lengthy detour in Haran. According to Acts 7:2, God spoke to Abram "while he was still in Mesopotamia, before he lived in Haran."

Leave ... and go ... I will show you. God called Abram to a major step of faith as well as a major lifestyle change. Abram was a middle-aged man, very prosperous, settled in his daily life, and living in a pagan land. He was basically asked to leave everything he had known (his country, his people, and his father's household) and enter into a totally unfamiliar situation to worship a God that very few people even acknowledged. Not only was everything in his life changing, he did not even know what to expect after the change was accomplished.

GENESIS 12:2–3

I will make ... I will bless. God's tremendous command to Abram comes in the form of a seven-fold promise: (1) great nation; (2) personal blessing; (3) great name; (4) blessings to others; (5) extended blessings; (6) extended protection; (7) universal blessing. God turned His attention to one man through whom a special nation would arise. Ultimately, the Messiah would come out of His new nation, and all peoples on earth would be blessed.

GENESIS 12:4

So Abram left, as the Lord had told him. Abram was a man of faith (Heb. 11:8). When God called him to leave the known behind and press forward into the unknown, he obeyed. He was "going, not knowing" what lay ahead. Yet, he trusted the One who was guiding him and preparing the way before him.

GENESIS 12:5

He took his wife ... his nephew ... possessions ... people. We can already see the evidence of the abundant blessing of God upon Abram's life. The phrase, "the people they had acquired," can also be translated "souls acquired." Part of the blessing that Abram was to be to others was as a witness to the true and living God. Abram's life and testimony would impact and influence countless others as he sought to follow his Lord's leading.

in Haran. A temporary stop on the way from Ur to Canaan.

they set out ... they arrived. Abram literally "pulled up the stakes" and moved onward to an uncertain future. Everything in his life had changed, except the one unchangeable truth that became his anchor of stability—a trustworthy, unchanging, and ever-present God! This was only one of many changes Abram would face in the years ahead, but the Scripture says he remained confident because "he considered him faithful who had made the promise" (Heb. 11:11).

10

notes

The Stress of Unfulfilled Expectations

Prepare for the Session

	READINGS	REFLECTIVE QUESTIONS
Monday	Philippians 4:10–13	On a scale of 1 (not at all) to 10 (completely), how content are you today? What is Paul's secret to contentment?
Tuesday	Hebrews 13:5	How much of your stress is due to worries about money? How does this verse comfort you?
Wednesday	1 Timothy 6:6–8	To what extent is your contentment based on your possessions?
Thursday	Psalm 63:1–5	How does David find satisfaction for his soul?
Friday	2 Corinthians 4:7–9	What circumstances are causing discontentment in your life today? How do you need God's "all-surpassing power"?
Saturday	Philippians 3:7–9	What secret to contentment is revealed here?
Sunday	Matthew 6:19–21	Where is the focus of your heart today?

BIBLE STUDY

- to understand that contentment is learned behavior
- to recognize that contentment does not dwell on comparisons
- to realize that contentment does not depend upon circumstances

LIFE CHANGE

- to make a list of unfulfilled goals and accept disappointment but not despair
- to make a list of new goals based on current circumstances
- to celebrate the special people, places, and moments in our lives

Icebreaker

10-15 minutes

GATHERING THE PEOPLE ♨ **Form horseshoe groups of 6–8.**

The Good Old Days and Wouldn't It Be Grand? Complete the following four statements and share your responses.

THE GOOD OLD DAYS

They just don't make TV shows like _____ anymore.

You can keep today's popular music. _____ (solo artist or group) will always be my favorite.

WOULDN'T IT BE GRAND?

Life would be sweet if I was driving a _____.

I sure wouldn't mind trading places with _____ for a week!

Information to Remember: In the spaces provided, take note of information you will need as you participate in this group in the weeks to come.

PEOPLE:

1. A person in the group (besides the leader) I learned from this week was:

2. A person who lifted my spirits was:

EVENTS: An event that is coming up that I want to make sure I am part of is _____. It will be _____ (time) on _____ (date) at _____ (location).

And if I have time, I would also like to be part of _____. It will be _____ (time) on _____ (date) at _____ (location).

Bible Study

30-45 minutes

The Scripture for this week:

LEARNING FROM THE BIBLE

PHILIPPIANS 4:10–13

¹⁰*I rejoice greatly in the Lord that at last you have renewed your concern for me. Indeed, you have been concerned, but you had no opportunity to show it.* ¹¹*I am not saying this because I am in need, for I have learned to be content whatever the circumstances.* ¹²*I know what it is to be in need, and I know what it is to have plenty. I have learned the secret of being content in any and every situation, whether well fed or hungry, whether living in plenty or in want.* ¹³*I can do everything through him who gives me strength.*

...about today's session

A WORD FROM THE LEADER

Write your answers here.

1. Who is a worthy mentor to teach us about contentment?

2. What was his goal? Where did he find himself instead?

Identifying with the Story

11

♘ In horseshoe groups of 6–8, explore questions as time allows.

1. How would you rate your present level of contentment?

1 · · 2 · · 3 · · 4 · · 5 · · 6 · · 7 · · 8 · · 9 · · 10

| | | | | |
life stinks   it's been better   no complaints   content   life is great

2. If you were in prison as the apostle Paul was, what do you think your attitude might be?

   ☐ So, this is the reward for following Christ?
   ☐ This jail stinks; this food stinks; these guards really stink—life stinks!
   ☐ I should have remained a Pharisee.
   ☐ I'll suffer through it.
   ☐ I want to call my lawyer.
   ☐ I'd rather die than be stuck in here.
   ☐ With God's help, I'll survive one day at a time.
   ☐ I love Jesus but He must not love me.
   ☐ These conditions are worse than *Survivor* and I won't make a dime.
   ☐ Other:_____

3. Which of the following reflects an area with which you are discontent?

   ☐ leisure time   ☐ physical health   ☐ car
   ☐ singleness   ☐ physical appearance   ☐ career
   ☐ childlessness   ☐ housing/geography   ☐ finances
   ☐ friendships   ☐ parenting/children
   ☐ marriage   ☐ other:_____

today's session

What is God teaching you from this story?

1. Before we define contentment, let's pause to clear up two misconceptions about contentment.

   a. Contentment is not _____.

   b. Contentment allows for _____.

2. Next, let's consider two things that contentment does not do.

   a. Contentment does not _____ on _____. What are the three deadly comparisons?

   ❖ What I have vs. what I _____ have.
   ❖ What I have now vs. what I _____ had.
   ❖ What I have vs. what _____ have.

   b. Contentment does not _____ upon _____.

✧ What is the hidden belief of discontentment?

✧ Contentment is the fruit of _____.

3. Finally, let's consider the process of contentment.

   a. Paul reveals a secret: Contentment is _____ behavior.

   b. What are some things that Paul learned?

      ✧ Paul learned to trust God's _____.
      ✧ Paul learned to extract _____ in the midst of difficulty.
      ✧ Paul learned to find causes for _____.

Learning from the Story

♆ In horseshoe groups of 6–8, choose an answer and explain why you chose what you did.

Take turns completing the following statements.

1. I'm especially relieved that contentment (choose one):

   ☐ does not mean I have to give up my hopes, goals, or dreams.
   ☐ does not mean I cannot wish things were different.
   ☐ does not mean I should never be disappointed or angry.
   ☐ does not mean having to always appear happy.

2. The comparison trap to which I am most susceptible is:

   ☐ what I have vs. what I should have.
   ☐ what I have now vs. what I once had.
   ☐ what I have vs. what others have.

3. If I've been operating from any misbelief concerning contentment, it is probably that I cannot possibly be happy unless/because

   _____.

4. If contentment is learned behavior, then ... (Check all that apply.)

   ☐ I need to be in a remedial class.
   ☐ I need to unlearn some wrong ways of thinking.
   ☐ I must commit myself to my education.
   ☐ I'm encouraged that contentment is attainable.
   ☐ I must not wait for my circumstances to change.
   ☐ I'm afraid I've not been paying attention in class.
   ☐ I can see some progress from a few years ago.
   ☐ Other:_____

11

life change lessons

How can you apply this session to your life?

Write your answers here.

1. Contentment allows for _____, but it does not give in to immobilizing _____.

2. You must learn to live in your _____.

   ✧ What is a sign that you are not learning a new language of contentment?

3. _____ the special people, places, and moments in your life.

   ✧ How can you explore the current place and season you're in?

Caring Time
15-20 minutes

CARING TIME

⟲ Remain in horseshoe groups of 6–8.

Take time to care for one another through prayer. Pray that each group member will learn, as Paul did, to be content in any situation. Also remember to include prayer for the concerns listed on the Prayer/Praise Report.

Pray specifically for God to guide you to someone to invite next week to fill the empty chair.

Conclude your prayer time by reading together the words of David in Psalm 63:1–5:

> O God, you are my God,
>   earnestly I seek you;
> my soul thirsts for you,
>   my body longs for you,
> in a dry and weary land
>   where there is no water.
>
> I have seen you in the sanctuary
>   and beheld your power and your glory.
> Because your love is better than life,
>   my lips will glorify you.
> I will praise you as long as I live,
>   and in your name I will lift up my hands.
> My soul will be satisfied as with the richest of foods;
>   with singing lips my mouth will praise you.

Reference Notes

Use these notes to gain further understanding
of the text as you study on your own.

Paul, writing from a Roman jail (Phil. 1:13), had just encouraged his Philippian readers to rejoice in the Lord (4:4), and to enjoy the incomprehensible peace of God (4:7). He now turns his attention from the gifts of joy and peace to the blessing of a contented heart.

PHILIPPIANS 4:10

I rejoice greatly in the Lord. The theme of joy is prevalent throughout the epistle to the Philippians. Paul rejoices (*chairo*) in the way God has blessed him through the expression of love and concern by the Philippian believers. Rather than focusing on what he lacks, Paul rejoices that there is one thing he never lacks—the abiding, comforting presence of Almighty God!

PHILIPPIANS 4:11

I am not saying this because I am in need. Paul did not beg, plead, or pressure others to assist his labors for Christ. He simply let the need be known and then trusted that God would amply provide (Phil. 4:18).

I have learned. The Greek word used here for *learned* is *manthano*, meaning to learn by use or practice, to acquire the habit of or to become accustomed to. Paul learned how to be content through first-hand experience.

content whatever the circumstances. Paul had learned a source of contentment totally independent of any circumstance or situation. The word *contentment* (*autarkes*) refers here to a divinely empowered sufficiency in all situations. Proverbs 19:23 says, "The fear of the Lord leads to life: Then one rests content, untouched by trouble." This is not to say that trouble never comes into the life of a Christian because Jesus, Himself, teaches that trouble is an expected part of earthly living (John 16:33). However, when the Lord is given full control of our lives, we can rest in contentment and confidence because He will not allow trouble to overcome us.

PHILIPPIANS 4:12

learned the secret. This phrase is literally translated "to initiate into the mysteries." It was like being given the critical clue to solving a difficult puzzle. Paul now understood the source of true contentment, as well as his part in obtaining it.

in any and every situation. Paul had experienced times of financial and material need as well as times of abundance. He wrote in 1 Timothy 6:6–8 about the benefits of remaining content with whatever we have and in whatever situation we find ourselves (see also Heb. 13:5).

PHILIPPIANS 4:13

I can do everything through him. Immediately after telling his readers he had learned the secret of contentment, Paul revealed the secret: his relationship with Christ! The phrase "gives me strength" is from the Greek word *endunamoo*, meaning to empower or enable. He can remain content regardless of circumstances because of his union with and submission to Christ.

11

notes

12

The Stress of Decision Making

Prepare for the Session

	READINGS	REFLECTIVE QUESTIONS
Monday	Psalm 23:1–4	What decisions are causing you stress? How can the Good Shepherd help you, according to these verses?
Tuesday	James 1:5–8	When you're seeking guidance, who is the first one you should ask? Who do you usually consult first?
Wednesday	Proverbs 3:5–6	How often do you acknowledge the Lord during your daily activities?
Thursday	Proverbs 11:14	When making tough decisions, do you seek feedback from "many advisers"?
Friday	Proverbs 16:9	What does this say about the sovereignty of God in your decision making?
Saturday	Acts 16:6–10	When have you felt a special guidance from God?
Sunday	Philippians 4:6–7	What is your first line of defense against the anxiety of decision making?

12

BIBLE STUDY
- to expose some questionable methods of decision making
- to understand the four distinct ways that God guides us
- to consider a biblical decision-making method that combines God's sovereignty with our freedom to choose

LIFE CHANGE
- to establish a regular prayer time
- to make informed decisions through research
- to seek godly counsel

Icebreaker

10-15 minutes

**GATHERING
THE PEOPLE
☰ Form
horseshoe
groups of 6–8.**

Take Your Pick. Review the story below and select one option from each pair or list of items in parentheses. Go around the group and have each person tell his or her story according to their selections.

It is *(winter/spring/summer/fall)* in *(California/Colorado/ Florida/Vermont)*. I *(wake up early/sleep in)* and *(go work out/ enjoy my coffee and newspaper)*. For breakfast I have a *(sesame seed bagel/ the Denny's Grand Slam)*. I drive my *(1994 BMW convertible/2001 Ford Explorer)* to work at *(Joe's Bait Shop and Sushi Bar/the Driver's License Bureau)*. While at work my mind wanders and I imagine *(being on the beach in Cancun/being on the slopes in Aspen)*. The highlight of the morning was the vending machine giving me a free *(Snickers Bar/Diet Coke)*. That was until I got the phone call that I was picked to be a contestant on *(The Weakest Link/Who Wants to Be a Millionaire?)*. It turned out to be *(a good friend/my ex-spouse)* playing a joke on me. That's okay, I'll get even by *(signing them up for the Never-Ending Music Club/junior high camp counselor)*.

Information to Remember: Finish the following sentences as you look around at the people here today.

1. A person here I would like to get to know better is:

2. A person who has really been a blessing to me during these sessions is:

Bible Study
30-45 minutes

The Scripture for this week:

[1]The Lord is my shepherd, I shall not be in want.
   [2]He makes me lie down in green pastures,
he leads me beside quiet waters,
   [3]he restores my soul.
He guides me in paths of righteousness
   for his name's sake.
[4]Even though I walk
   through the valley of the shadow of death,
I will fear no evil,
   for you are with me;
your rod and your staff,
   they comfort me.

...about today's session

**A WORD
FROM THE
LEADER**

1. How is the final scene of the movie *Castaway* a life metaphor?

**Write your
answers
here.**

2. What is our basic fear in decision making?

12

3. How large is the scope of impact from our decision making?

4. In decision making, what do we want to receive from God?

Identifying with the Story

☙ In
horseshoe
groups
of 6–8,
explore
questions as
time allows.

1. When you read or hear Psalm 23, what do you immediately think about?

   ☐ funeral service
   ☐ picture of a shepherd with a lamb in his lap
   ☐ a great passage to cross-stitch and frame for my grandmother
   ☐ other:_____

2. What are some things a shepherd does for his sheep?

3. In what key area(s) are you facing a decision right now?

   ☐ relationship issues   ☐ career issues
   ☐ parenting issues   ☐ education issues
   ☐ financial issues   ☐ health issues
   ☐ spiritual issues   ☐ other:_____

4. What would you say is the most difficult decision you have ever faced?

today's session

1. What are the functions of a shepherd as it relates to us in the stress of our decision making?

2. How is deism opposed to the Bible's teaching about God?

3. What are some questionable approaches to decision making?

    1. Putting out the _____.

    2. Looking for a _____.

    3. _____ Scripture.

    4. Requesting a solitary _____.

    5. Giving the _____ sign.

4. According to Garry Friesen, what are the four distinct ways that God guides?

    M _____ Guidance

    W _____ Guidance

    S _____ Guidance

    S _____ Guidance

5. What are the four principles of God's guidance and decision making according to Friesen?

    a. Where God commands, we must _____ (God's moral will).

    b. Where there is no command, we are morally _____ _____ (God-given freedom).

    c. In the area of freedom, we must use godly _____.

    d. Trust everything else into God's _____ hands.

12

111

Learning from the Story

In horseshoe groups of 6–8, choose an answer and explain why you chose what you did.

1. Which of these questionable methods of decision making have you tried?

   ☐ putting out the fleece   ☐ requesting a solitary door
   ☐ looking for a sign   ☐ giving the peace sign
   ☐ hijacking Scripture

2. Which of the following statements describes your feelings about decision making and the will of God?

   ☐ I'd prefer that He'd leave me alone and let me decide.
   ☐ I wish He'd take me by the hand and walk me through the right door.
   ☐ I prefer to think that God has a bull's-eye in the target for me to hit.
   ☐ I wish He'd send a blueprint for my entire life.
   ☐ I wish He'd give me complete freedom but stop me if I'm about to do something really stupid.
   ☐ I wish we could at least play "Hot or Cold." You know, hear Him say, "You're getting warmer, WARMER ... oh, now you're getting cooler."

3. How should God's sovereignty reduce the sense of pressure we often feel to hit the bull's-eye in flawless decision making?

4. How does thinking of the Lord as your Good Shepherd encourage you as you face decisions?

112

life change lessons

1. Establish a regular _____ time. What should you pray and ask for?

2. Make informed decisions through _____. How is this step compatible with trusting God?

3. Seek godly _____. What are two types of counselors you should seek out?

Caring Time

15-20 minutes

Go around the group and have each member pray for the person on his or her left. Pray especially for God's wisdom and guidance in any decisions this group member needs to make. Pray, also, that everyone will find peace in the security of God's sovereignty. Remember to include prayer for the concerns listed on the Prayer/Praise Report.

Pray specifically for God to guide you to someone to invite next week to fill the empty chair.

12

Reference Notes

Use these notes to gain further understanding
of the text as you study on your own.

**PSALM
23:1**

The Lord is my shepherd. The author of this psalm, David, uses the image of a shepherd to describe the blessings he has enjoyed from the Lord as well as the assurance he has for the future. The word *shepherd* is the Hebrew word *raah*, meaning to tend, to keep, or to rule a flock. This psalm is a profession of the trust of the shepherd-king (David) in his Good Shepherd (the Lord).

I shall not be in want. I want (chacer) means lacking, going without, or in need. David is expressing his confidence in and his satisfaction with God's provision for his life.

**PSALM
23:2**

He makes me lie down. The Good Shepherd (John 10:1–8) does not force His sheep to lie down. Rather, He makes them lie down (*nathan*, from the root word "to give" or "to cause"), in the sense of caring so well for them that they are completely content. A hungry sheep would never lie down (*rabats*, meaning to recline, repose, or rest) in a green pasture because he would need to feed his hunger. In like manner, the Lord desires to fill our hearts and lives with such abundance that we can rest contentedly in our "pastures" (*naah*, meaning pleasant places).

he leads me ... he restores. Our Good Shepherd leads us (Isa. 40:11) to places of quiet waters (restful waters that provide renewal and refreshment). He restores (*shuwb*, meaning to turn back, to recover, to rescue) our soul. The word *soul* (*nephesh*) refers to the total person—mind, body, and overall vitality.

**PSALM
23:3**

He guides me. One of the shepherd's main duties is to lead his flock to places of provision, abundance, and safety (Ps. 78:72; John 10:3–4,9). Interestingly enough, the word guide is literally translated as "to run with a sparkle." It means to protect, to carry, to sustain, and to lead on gently.

righteousness for his name's sake. Righteousness (*tsedeq*) can be translated in this passage as either that which is morally and legally right, or it can mean "in the way of prosperity." Both the moral living and the prosperity (material and/or spiritual) of God's servants bring honor to the Lord's name (Jer. 14:21).

**PSALM
23:4**

Even though I walk through ... fear no evil. The psalmist acknowledges that sometimes the circumstances of life are difficult, but that even in the midst of facing unknown outcomes, he is not afraid of any evil that lies ahead (*ra*, meaning adversity, affliction, calamity, grief, harm, or trouble). *you are with me.* These words are the heart of the psalm. God never lets go, and He never forsakes us. He is our ever-present companion in any and all situations (Ps. 46:1–3). This was the source of David's confidence that saw him through, even when the Lord led him into the valleys of his life. *your rod ... your staff ... comfort me.* The shepherd's rod was used to guide, correct, protect, rescue, and even count the sheep to make certain none were lost. The shepherd's staff was an instrument of support and stability. The psalmist found great comfort in the presence, the strength, and the guidance of his Lord.

12

notes

The Stress of Monotony

Prepare for the Session

	READINGS	REFLECTIVE QUESTIONS
Monday	Exodus 16:35	How would you feel about eating the same food every day for 40 years?
Tuesday	Numbers 11:4–9	When have you felt the stress of monotony in your life?
Wednesday	Galatians 6:9	What blessings come from the daily, sometimes boring, tasks you do?
Thursday	Psalm 36:5–7	Take time to praise God for His daily faithfulness and love.
Friday	Matthew 24:42–47	How can you continue to be a "faithful and wise servant" until Jesus comes?
Saturday	2 Corinthians 4:16–18	What new meaning could your daily routine have if you fixed your eyes on what is eternal?
Sunday	Luke 5:15–16	How did prayer help Jesus cope with everyday life? How can you follow His example today?

BIBLE STUDY
- to recognize God's gift of consistency
- to understand how striving for secular greatness can destroy relationships
- to appreciate how the greatness that comes through servanthood enhances relationships

LIFE CHANGE
- to plan one way to alter our routines in the nonspiritual areas of our lives
- to design a new "workout routine" to breathe fresh life into our spiritual disciplines
- to select one new way this week to experience authentic Christian friendship, service to others, or telling others about Jesus

Icebreaker

10-15 minutes

Guardians of the Group. We have a lot of guardians in the world that protect us from many kinds of dangers. Even this group has had its "guardians." In silence, decide which person in the group best fulfilled each of the following roles for you. After everyone has made their decisions, focus on one group member at a time and have the others report the role they chose for that person.

HEART MONITOR: the one who kept the group alive by keeping in touch with the heart

TRAIL GUIDE: the one who brought us back when we wandered from the path

CLASS CLOWN. the one who helped us keep our sense of humor

"CHILD" WHO GUIDES US TO THE KINGDOM: the one who protected our innocence and childlike faith

GUARDIAN ANGEL: the one whose loving protection seemed to come from God

MOTHER HEN: the one whose gift of hospitality made us feel well taken care of

Information to Remember: Finish the following sentences as you look around at the people here today.

1. A person I would like to hear from more today is:

2. A person God is leading me to say something special to today is:

Bible Study

30-45 minutes

The Scripture for this week:

³⁵*The Israelites ate manna forty years, until they came to a land that was settled; they ate manna until they reached the border of Canaan.*

⁴*The rabble with them began to crave other food, and again the Israelites started wailing and said, "If only we had meat to eat!* ⁵*We remember the fish we ate in Egypt at no cost—also the cucumbers, melons, leeks, onions and garlic.* ⁶*But now we have lost our appetite; we never see anything but this manna!"*

⁷*The manna was like coriander seed and looked like resin.* ⁸*The people went around gathering it, and then ground it in a handmill or crushed it in a mortar. They cooked it in a pot or made it into cakes. And it tasted like something made with olive oil.* ⁹*When the dew settled on the camp at night, the manna also came down.*

...about today's session

A WORD
FROM THE
LEADER

Write your
answers
here.

1. What are the two "friends" that frequently accompany boredom?

13

2. Sketch the difference between you as a "system" vs. "compartments."

3. What are the implications of the "systems" approach for overcoming spiritual boredom?

Identifying with the Story

**In
horseshoe
groups
of 6–8,
explore
questions as
time allows.**

1. What is a food you really enjoy but would definitely not want to eat every day?

2. What area of your life is really in a rut?

- [ ] what I do after work
- [ ] what we do after the kids go to bed
- [ ] my morning routine
- [ ] prayer
- [ ] my lunch hour
- [ ] weekend plans
- [ ] devotional reading
- [ ] exercise
- [ ] other: _____

3. Which of the following words describe you? (Feel free to choose more than one.)

- ☐ predictable
- ☐ reliable
- ☐ innovative
- ☐ consistent
- ☐ undisciplined
- ☐ flexible
- ☐ spontaneous
- ☐ organized
- ☐ disciplined
- ☐ traditional
- ☐ creative
- ☐ compliant

today's session

What is God teaching you from this story?

1. What is the role of consistency in your spiritual life?

2. What is the possible flip side of consistency?

3. What two aspects of God reveal His variety and creativity?

    a. God as our _____.

    b. God as the _____ _____.

Learning from the Story

⟲ **In horseshoe groups of 6–8, choose an answer and explain why you chose what you did.**

1. How would you describe your current practice of spiritual disciplines?

- ☐ I'm not even showing up for practice.
- ☐ I'm sporadic at best.
- ☐ I'm floundering for lack of a workable plan.
- ☐ I'm enjoying some recent consistency.
- ☐ I'm enjoying consistency and variety.
- ☐ I'm fairly consistent but not getting much out of it.
- ☐ I'm consistent but digging a rut.
- ☐ Other:_____

13

2. Perhaps the major contributor to my spiritual boredom is:

☐ my lack of creativity and spontaneity with life in general
☐ mistakenly thinking that all God cares about is obedience
☐ failing to understand that God wants me to enjoy my relationship with Him
☐ not recognizing that, as the Creator, God obviously employs variety
☐ not recognizing that, as the Master Communicator, God has demonstrated creativity throughout the Bible

3. How has God demonstrated His creativity when communicating His message?

life change lessons

How can you apply this session to your life?

Write your answers here.

1. Plan one way to alter your routine in the _____ areas of your life. What are some practical and creative things you can do to get out of your daily rut?

2. Design a new _____ _____ to breathe fresh life into your spiritual disciplines. What are some practical and creative interventions you might like to try?

3. Select one new way this week to experience _____, _____, or _____. What are you willing to try?

Caring Time

15-20 minutes

Pray for the concerns listed on the Prayer/Praise Report, then continue with the evaluation and covenant.

1. Take some time to evaluate the life of your group by using the statements below. Read the first sentence out loud and ask everyone to explain where they would put a dot between the two extremes. When you are finished, go back and give your group an overall grade in the categories of Group Building, Bible Study, and Mission.

 GROUP BUILDING

On celebrating life and having fun together, we were more like a …
wet blanket · hot tub

On becoming a caring community, we were more like a …
prickly porcupine · cuddly teddy bear

 BIBLE STUDY

On sharing our spiritual stories, we were more like a …
shallow pond · spring-fed lake

On digging into Scripture, we were more like a …
slow-moving snail · · · · · · · · · · · · · · · · · · · voracious anteater

 MISSION

On inviting new people into our group, we were more like a …
barbed-wire fence · wide-open door

On stretching our vision for mission, we were more like an …
ostrich · eagle

13

2. What are some specific areas in which you have grown in this course?

- ☐ worrying less and praying more
- ☐ learning from failure and making appropriate adjustments
- ☐ resolving conflicts and seeking reconciliation when possible
- ☐ reducing job stress and evaluating job compatibility
- ☐ making time for a Sabbath rest
- ☐ offering support to others in times of crisis
- ☐ clinging to God during times of change
- ☐ learning to be content in spite of circumstances
- ☐ seeking godly counsel when making decisions
- ☐ other: _____

A covenant is a promise made to another in the presence of God. Its purpose is to indicate your intention to make yourselves available to one another for the fulfillment of the purposes you share in common. If your group is going to continue, in a spirit of prayer work your way through the following sentences, trying to reach an agreement on each statement pertaining to your ongoing life together. Write out your covenant like a contract, stating your purpose, goals, and the ground rules for your group.

1. The purpose of our group will be:

2. Our goals will be:

3. We will meet on _____ (day of week).

4. We will meet for _____weeks, after which we will decide if we wish to continue as a group.

5. We will meet from _____ to _____ and we will strive to start on time and end on time.

6. We will meet at _____ (place) or we will rotate from house to house.

7. We will agree to the following ground rules for our group (check):

☐ **PRIORITY:** While you are in this course of study, you give the group meetings priority.

☐ **PARTICIPATION:** Everyone is encouraged to participate and no one dominates.

☐ **RESPECT:** Everyone has the right to his or her own opinion, and all questions are encouraged and respected.

☐ **CONFIDENTIALITY:** Anything said in the meeting is never repeated outside the meeting.

☐ **LIFE CHANGE:** We will regularly assess our own life change goals and encourage one another in our pursuit of Christlikeness.

☐ **EMPTY CHAIR:** The group stays open to reaching new people at every meeting.

☐ **CARE and SUPPORT:** Permission is given to call upon each other at any time especially in times of crisis. The group will provide care for every member.

☐ **ACCOUNTABILITY:** We agree to let the members of the group hold us accountable to the commitments which each of us make in whatever loving ways we decide upon.

☐ **MISSION:** We will do everything in our power to start a new group.

☐ **MINISTRY:** The group will encourage one another to volunteer and serve in a ministry, and to support missions by giving financially and/or personally serving.

13

Reference Notes

Use these notes to gain further understanding
of the text as you study on your own.

One year earlier, the Israelites had been delivered from Egyptian bondage through the waters of the Red Sea. Only three days into their journey beyond the Red Sea, the Israelites were grumbling and complaining to Moses about the lack of water (Ex. 15:22–27). For a full year after that experience, the Lord taught His people the precious Word of God at Mount Sinai, and they learned to follow the Lord's leading day-by-day (Num. 9:15–23). Now, a year later, the Israelites were leaving Sinai on their way to the land that God had promised them. Once again, only three days into the journey the people began to grumble. This time, however, their complaints focused on their desires rather than their needs.

EXODUS 16:35

The Israelites ate manna forty years. Deuteronomy 8:2–3 indicates that the manna was part of God's plan to humble the Israelites and to test them to reveal the condition of their hearts. In similar fashion, the Lord will often take us through a prolonged period of waiting or a lengthy season of trials and difficulties to purify our hearts and to prepare us for receiving a tailor-made blessing. Only by submitting ourselves daily to the Lord's control and strength are we able to remain humble, obedient, and faithful in the waiting room of monotony.

NUMBERS 11:4

The rabble ... crave ... the Israelites started wailing. The rabble (*asapsup*, meaning collection) referred to the mixed multitude of non-Israelites who accompanied Israel during their exodus from Egypt. The rabble began to crave (*taavah*, meaning to long for, to lust after, or to exceedingly desire) something other than the Lord's provision. Their discontent spread like a cancer into the minds and hearts of the Lord's people. God's people began wailing (*bakah*, meaning to bemoan, to complain, to lament, or to mourn) before the Lord.

NUMBERS 11:5–6

We remember ... at no cost ... lost our appetite. The longing of the people turned from what lay ahead for them in God's plan to what they had left behind in order to follow Him. The "waiting game" was taking its toll on the ranks as they became more and more dissatisfied with the monotony of their present circumstances. The phrase, "lost our appetite," comes from the Hebrew word *yahesh* meaning disappointed, dried up (as water), or withered away. Eager to mentally escape their daily routine, they even fantasized about the life they once "enjoyed" in Egypt. They

NUMBERS
11:5–6
(cont'd)

recalled the variety of foods available to them at no cost (*chinnam*, meaning without monetary cost). They had blocked from their memories the true and extreme price they had paid daily for this "free" food—the harsh and unending, backbreaking toil of forced labor. Sometimes, in the struggle of our daily routines, we develop this type of "selective memory"; we forget all that God has done for us and all that He has planned for us. The ability to see, to appreciate, and to focus on the blessings of God in our lives is one key to rising above the weariness of feeling stuck in a daily holding pattern.

NUMBERS
11:7

The manna. When the manna first appeared in Exodus 16:13–16, the people named it *manhu*, meaning, "What is it?" It settled on the ground in the form of thin flakes, white like coriander seeds, and it looked like resin—perhaps sticky in texture. The manna was a supernatural, miraculous provision of the Lord to supply the physical needs of His people. Nothing like it had ever been seen before, nor has it been seen since the day the Israelites entered the promised land (Josh. 5:12). Only a small sample of manna was preserved to provide a testimony of the Lord's faithfulness to future generations (Ex. 16:32–34).

NUMBERS
11:8

gathering it ... ground it ... crushed it ... cooked it ... made it. These phrases indicate that daily life for the Israelites revolved around manna. Because it was supplied on a daily basis and would not last until the next day (except on the Sabbath—Ex. 16:22–26), the people had to gather, prepare, and partake of God's provision each day.

NUMBERS
11:9

When the dew settled ... the manna also came. Just as surely as the dew settled on the ground each night, the Lord's faithfulness to His people was evident each new morning as the Israelites awoke to find the food they needed to live.

13

**PASS THIS DIRECTORY AROUND AND
HAVE YOUR GROUP MEMBERS FILL IN
THEIR NAMES AND PHONE NUMBERS.**

Group Directory

NAME

PHONE